ZOO TYCOON™

Michael Rymaszewski

SAN FRANCISCO · PARIS · DÜSSELDORF · LONDON

W9-BAH-321

ASSOCIATE PUBLISHER: DAN BRODNITZ

CONTRACTS AND LICENSING MANAGER: KRISTINE O'CALLAGHAN

ACQUISITIONS AND DEVELOPMENTAL EDITOR: WILLEM KNIBBE

EDITOR: BILL CASSEL

PRODUCTION EDITOR: KELLY WINQUIST

PROOFREADER: RICH GANIS

BOOK DESIGN: DIANA VAN WINKLE, VAN WINKLE DESIGN

BOOK PRODUCTION: DIANA VAN WINKLE, VAN WINKLE DESIGN

POSTER LAYOUT: DIANA VAN WINKLE, VAN WINKLE DESIGN

POSTER ART: THE BLUE FANG ART TEAM

COVER DESIGN: VICTOR ARRE

ISBN: 0-7821-4042-4

Manufactured in the United States of America

10 9 8 7 6 5 4 3 2 1

Acknowledgments

A published book is always a collective effort. Many big thanks are due to Willem Knibbe and Kelly Winquist at Sybex, who actually made this into a book; to Bill Cassel, whose editing skill made it much more readable; and to Diana Van Winkle, thanks to whom everything looks as nice as it does.

Separate thanks are owed to Dana Fos, Charlie Peterson, and Eric Haddock at Microsoft, who tirelessly reviewed the text until everything was put right. The outstanding support received from Blue Fang, the game's developer, is another story. Designer Adam Levesque and fellow Blue Fangs Mark Kolenski, Shawn Stone, and John Wheeler not only reviewed and corrected the text, but also supplied data tables and patiently answered countless and often silly questions.

Finally, a personal thank you to Michael Krotowski, whose timely technical assistance made things easier; and to Winston Cooper for his soothing influence.

ONTENTS

CHAPTER **3**

THE ZOO ANIMALS 36

CHAPTER **4**

THE ZOO PEOPLE 82

CHAPTER **5**

ZOO EVOLUTION............ 96

CHAPTER **6**

THE BEST ZOO IN THE WORLD 118

CHAPTER **7**

MAKING MONEY. 136

INTRODUCTION

So you're to be the ultimate zoo big shot, eh? You must have what it takes to successfully manage dozens of wild animals. And of course you also know how to make people so happy that they'll gladly stuff your pockets with their hard-earned money. But everyone has bad days (it's rumored even the gods do); and when you're having a bad day in your tycoon career, this book will help you. Needless to say, it will also help anyone who just wants to polish their *Zoo Tycoon* abilities.

This book's structure reflects the structure of the game. As explained in Chapter 1, winning at *Zoo Tycoon* involves mastering several skills. If you're familiar with city-building games, you'll enjoy an advantage from the start: a lot of *Zoo Tycoon*'s gameplay consists of planning and building things. You'll have to do everything from designing zoo exhibits to strategically positioning restrooms. But other skills come into play, too, and Chapter 1 enumerates them while explaining what it takes to win.

The book's remaining chapters discuss, in detail, the concepts and issues introduced in Chapter 1. Chapter 2 is about zoo design and design execution; among other things, it identifies considerations that have to be resolved *before* you start building anything. It also contains a review of the numerous building options the game offers. Chapter 3, like your zoo, is devoted to animals. All the animals available for adoption in the game are discussed in some detail, with special emphasis on individual animal likes and dislikes.

Chapter 4 discusses the intricacies of managing both zoo staff and zoo guests to your best advantage, while Chapter 5 deals with zoo evolution. It discusses all of the factors involved in changing and expanding your zoo, paying special attention to zoo research. Chapter 6 focuses on what makes a zoo great, focusing on the factors that determine zoo rating and describing the awards you'll win once you get good at the game. Chapter 7 focuses on the "tycoon" part of the game, discussing everything that has anything to do with zoo finances. Finally, Chapter 8 contains walkthroughs for all of the game's set scenarios.

The book concludes with a set of appendices designed so that you can easily refer to them while playing the game. These appendices contain, in table form, valuable game data that will enable you to instantly evaluate the wisdom of any planned move.

We sincerely hope you'll enjoy this book as much as you find it useful.

IT'S A ZOO AND YOU'RE IN CHARGE!

ZOO TYCOON IS A GAME THAT REQUIRES YOU TO SUCCESS-FULLY CARE FOR AND MANAGE NEARLY 50 DIFFERENT SPECIES OF ANIMALS. THIS NUMBER INCLUDES HOMO SAPIENS—A SPECIES THAT'S NOTORIOUSLY DIFFICULT TO MANAGE AND WHOSE HAPPINESS MAY BE SECURED ONLY THROUGH HONEST EFFORT AND CEASELESS VIGILANCE. OH, AND YOU'RE EXPECTED TO MAKE TONS OF MONEY IN THE PROCESS, TOO.

THIS CHAPTER IS AN OVERVIEW OF ZOO TYCOON THAT DESCRIBES THE KEY THINGS YOU MUST DO TO WIN THE GAME, REGARDLESS OF WHETHER YOU'RE PLAYING A SCENARIO OR A FREEFORM GAME. FIRST WE'LL LOOK AT THE CRUCIAL ISSUE OF HAPPINESS—BOTH THE ANIMAL'S AND THE GUEST'S. THEN WE'LL CONSIDER ZOO AESTHETICS AND FINANCES. THE FINAL SECTIONS OF THIS CHAPTER WILL BRIEFLY REVIEW TECHNICAL ISSUES AND GAME INTERFACE FEATURES THAT MAY BE TRICKY FOR THE NEW GAMER. AFTER READING THIS CHAPTER, YOU WILL HAVE A GENERAL UNDERSTANDING OF HOW THE GAME WORKS; EACH KEY CONCEPT AND ISSUE WILL BE DISCUSSED IN DETAIL IN THE CHAPTERS THAT FOLLOW.

THE IMPORTANCE OF HAPPINESS

NOTE

In Zoo Tycoon, money and happiness enjoy a symbiotic relationship. Money buys happiness (through investments that make animals and zoo guests happy); and happiness makes money, just like that. A happy zoo is a profitable zoo. Trying to nickel-and-dime your way up to tycoon status is not a good idea.

As we all know from life, happiness is…happiness isn't easy. Well, your main goal—objective *numero uno*—in *Zoo Tycoon* is to make all the animals and all the people in your zoo happy. Objective number two is to *keep* everyone happy. And just as in life, it isn't easy. But that's why you acquired this wonderful guide, right?

Chapters 3, 4, and 6 of this guide discuss happiness in great detail, but here's the golden rule: to bring long-lasting happiness to all the creatures in your zoo, you must *concentrate on making the animals happy first!* Broadly speaking, if the animals are unhappy, all the other attractions in the world won't make up for it. If the animals are happy, so are the guests, even when they're tired, hungry, and thirsty and they need to get to the bathroom within the next 28 seconds. And of course it goes without saying that you're a sensitive, intelligent person and want the animals in your zoo as happy as possible (see Figure 1.1). They make you money, after all.

FIGURE 1.1:

Me one happy animal, you one happy tycoon.

MAKING ANIMALS HAPPY

The secret to making an animal happy lies in creating an exhibit that reproduces the animal's natural environment and fits its space and privacy needs. You must also provide the animal in your care with food and medical care (zookeeper) and appropriate exhibit maintenance (zookeeper, maintenance worker, and yourself). Be warned that some animals are much more choosy about their surroundings than others! It's harder to keep a relatively intelligent animal—such as an exotic cat or a species of monkey—happy. As a rule, herbivores adapt better than carnivores. Most animals need the companionship of other animals to be truly happy, and herbivores often like the companionship of other species (animals of the African savannah are a good example).

If you're successful at meeting the animals' needs, they'll usually reward you by reproducing. You might say that by giving birth, an animal in your care gives its ultimate stamp of approval to the way you're meeting its needs. It's good to remember that baby animals generate happiness all around, and also that they may be sold at a nice profit. This may sound cold-hearted, but keeping all those baby animals will ultimately lead to overcrowding and unhappiness. Every animal needs a certain amount of space for itself, as we'll discuss in Chapter 3.

MAKING PEOPLE HAPPY

The guests in your zoo came there for a purpose, didn't they? They came to see the animals. And they didn't come to see mangy, moth-eaten, sorrowful specimens; they like their animals bouncy and bushy-tailed. Yes, it's rule number one again: the first step to human happiness is animal happiness.

However, there's more to human happiness than that. People like beauty and will judge your zoo in aesthetic terms. An ugly zoo decreases guest happiness and zoo rating (see Chapter 6); as you would suspect, trashcans and trash

TIP

Put the animal information panel (which you bring up by clicking the chosen animal) to good use! Keep it open while fine-tuning a new exhibit, referring to the zookeeper's recommendations at regular intervals. The top bar on the panel shows animal happiness, and this bar must be green at all times. In Zoo Tycoon, keeping animals happy is always priority number one!

NOTE

You can research and subsequently construct Animal Houses: buildings that contain various forms of animal life (each counts as a zoo attraction). Providing information about the animals in your zoo may count as entertainment, too: Hiring zoo tour guides has a positive effect on guest happiness.

are an ugly sight, possibly leading to dark thoughts among the guests ("This zoo is dirty"). When you consider that happy guests mean more guests, which mean more trash, you'll quickly realize that things can get very complicated indeed. It's relatively easy to beautify your zoo with extra trees, flowerbeds, statues, fountains, etc., but a failure in trash control can render all your other efforts to improve zoo aesthetics null and void.

People also like to be entertained. While happy animals are the most important source of entertainment for your zoo's guests (you'll find the game's animations pretty entertaining yourself), you can provide additional attractions by investing in certain zoo buildings (for example, the animal theater or the carousel).

People also like to eat. Once they've eaten, they like to drink. And a short while after they've eaten and drank, they like to be able to perform a bit of private business (see Figure 1.2). You can view the guest information panel, which lists these basic needs, by clicking any of the people visiting your zoo. Chapters 4 and 6 discuss every aspect of guest happiness in detail.

FIGURE 1.2:
This little building is one of the most important structures in your zoo.

WHO ARE THOSE PEOPLE?

The people in your zoo are a diverse group. Chapter 4 discusses them in detail; here are just a few facts to help you see the big picture clearly.

To begin with, the people in your zoo fall into two categories: zoo employees and guests. As you know from the interface and the game manual, there are three kinds of employees:

Zookeepers take care of the animals and keep the exhibits clean. They must be able to get quickly to the exhibits under their care, so you should give extra thought to where you put the exhibit entrances. The performance of zookeepers improves after you've done appropriate research (as discussed in Chapters 4 and 6). At $800 a month, zookeepers are the best-paid zoo staff: their combined salaries have a significant impact on your zoo's budget. This will likely cause you difficulty at the start of every freeform game and in some scenarios; Chapters 4 and 7 provide relevant advice.

Maintenance workers keep the zoo clean of trash. They also repair exhibit fencing that has deteriorated, and this is where they really earn their wages! Replacing a single section of worn-out fencing may cost as much as $200 when you do it yourself, while a maintenance worker collects just $300 a month in salary and can easily repair 30+ fencing sections in a game month (as long as he isn't called away to do something else). You can improve the efficiency of your maintenance workers by conducting appropriate research.

Tour guides increase guest happiness by providing information about the exhibits. They are expensive at $500 a month and therefore are something of a luxury; it's wise to postpone hiring them until your zoo is firmly on its feet in the financial sense. Tour guides become more efficient once you've done relevant research.

The overwhelming majority of the people in your zoo will be zoo guests. (If that isn't so, you've made a very bad move somewhere!) Now, all those guests aren't created equal. If you zoom in while playing the game and watch them for a while, you'll quickly see that they come in four varieties: man, woman, boy, and girl. Each type of guest has his/her own preferences; what's more, adult guests (men and women) have different preferences from children. In addition, every guest has his/her own favorite animal (see Figure 1.3); seeing that animal in the zoo will greatly increase that guest's happiness. Making everyone happy can be quite a challenge! See Chapter 4 for more details.

FIGURE 1.3:
The guest information panel will tell you everything you need to know about the chosen guest.

ZOO DESIGN

Good zoo design involves a lot of imagination and foresight. The better you arrange everything, the more time guests will spend in your zoo; the longer they stay, the more they'll spend. Also, your design must anticipate the inevitable changes your zoo will go through when you play any but the shortest, easiest scenarios. And, of course, it goes without saying that you will design exhibits that make all your animals delirious with happiness.

You should always examine the map carefully before beginning construction. Quite often, the best course of action is to bulldoze everything (thus receiving some extra starting cash) and design your zoo from scratch. However, you'll also find that on occasion you can utilize the existing terrain and foliage for an exhibit, thus saving money. In some scenarios, a little money saved right at the start can mean a lot!

MAKING THEM STAY JUST A LITTLE BIT LONGER

The best way to prolong your guests' zoo visit is to make them walk everywhere, and then walk everywhere yet again. By placing exhibits and amenities just so, you can pull each guest along an invisible thread that runs into every nook and cranny of your zoo. Each animal has its own unique attractiveness rating, and you should consider this when deciding where to place individual exhibits. For instance, placing a highly attractive animal right by the entrance can be a major mistake: it makes people stay right by the entrance instead of moving on to explore your zoo. Placing the same exhibit a little farther on will make quite a few guests turn in that direction upon entering the zoo, reducing the front-gate congestion and hopefully putting them on a long journey through your entire zoo that will include several pit stops at assorted amenities, with a lot of dollars changing hands.

Chapter 2 offers an in-depth look at the intricacies of zoo design, and there's some extra advice in Chapters 5 and 6. The key rule is to make everything as spacious as possible so that your guests will have to walk a lot. Build large exhibits (see Figure 1.4), and run paths around them, leaving space between exhibit barriers and the path. This makes future additions and changes to your zoo easier. However, keep in mind that guests have to be within two tiles of the exhibit in order to view animals and that they have a sight range of just 10 tiles.

TIP

Building a large four-way, double-lane crossroads a few tiles away from the front entrance is almost invariably a very good move. The only exceptions to the rule are scenarios where space constraints render a big crossroads impractical, such as "Inner City Zoo."

FIGURE 1.4:

After walking around this lot, the guests will sure need a bite and a drink—ka-ching!

Don't bunch big attractions together; spread them out. It's best not to build your zoo exhibit by exhibit; try to have an idea of how several exhibits will work together as an area before you place even a single section of fencing.

The seating provided near buildings selling food and drinks usually doesn't suffice for all the tired guests; inserting rest areas between exhibit areas is a good move, especially since they may also feature a money-making building or two.

Don't panic if your investments in guest amenities don't start making money right away. It takes a guest over a month of game time to develop a healthy appetite! Indeed, when starting a new zoo, it makes sense not to build any amenities at all for a couple of months; almost all amenities require upkeep, and you'll save money if you postpone building them until the second or third month of your zoo's operation. Remember that you do not need to hire any maintenance workers in the first month, either.

WARNING

A single exhibit containing a single, happy animal is better than having ten exhibits with unhappy animals. There's no bigger turnoff for guests than to see sad, possibly sick animals. If you let things slide too far, you'll also be unable to get more animals for your zoo.

THE CHANGING ZOO

In all but the simplest scenarios, you'll be continuously improving and expanding your zoo. This is fully discussed in Chapter 5; here are a few general points to keep in mind.

A good, simple plan is to lay out the entrance crossroads (described earlier in "Making Them Stay Just a Little Bit Longer") right at the start. Each of the three paths spreading out from the entrance will eventually become very busy, necessitating the addition on an extra lane (sometimes even two for a triple-lane zoo highway). When things reach that stage, the empty space around the entrance will suddenly become extremely handy for extra guest amenities. You'll see numerous guests heading determinedly for the entrance/exit, then stopping by one of the amenities (or resting on a convenient bench) and subsequently beginning to tour the zoo once again!

Leave enough space between exhibits to allow for future double-lane paths. Make each exhibit extra large, and you'll always be able to cut it back by a row of tiles instead of having to bulldoze and rebuild it. Big exhibits allow the animals to reproduce happily without becoming crowded; they also need proportionally more foliage, rocks, etc. This is good news because placing a species' favorite foliage and rock types inside the exhibit boosts animal happiness: every item carries a small bonus. Of course, building big exhibits also has the added benefit of making your guests walk more right from the start, which leads to extra purchases of food and drinks.

Later scenarios and large-map freeform games are naturally more demanding. As a rule, try to leave plenty of open space both near the front gate and right in the center of the zoo. The central area should feature a big set of guest amenities (a restaurant is obligatory), including plenty of seating and attractions, such as an animal theater and carousel. These will ensure that guests naturally gravitate toward the center for refreshments and relief, after which they'll be happy to resume touring your zoo, spending more money in the process.

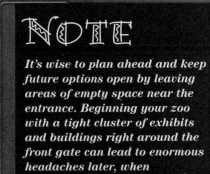

NOTE

It's wise to plan ahead and keep future options open by leaving areas of empty space near the entrance. Beginning your zoo with a tight cluster of exhibits and buildings right around the front gate can lead to enormous headaches later, when monthly zoo attendance is well into three figures. You may have no choice but to bulldoze several exhibits and build them anew!

BEAUTY AND THE BEASTS

Happiness depends to a large extent on the way one perceives things. So it's no wonder that zoo aesthetics affect your guests' happiness in a meaningful way.

Beauty is said to lie in the eye of the beholder, and this certainly is true in *Zoo Tycoon*. Every type of guest—man, woman, boy, and girl—has his/her own aesthetic preferences. For example, the hard solidity of a decorative iron fence will have a special appeal to males of all ages, but females prefer the peaceful appeal of a white picket fence. These specific preferences apply to virtually everything in your zoo, including the exhibits and animal houses. Only a boy can find special beauty among Scorpions of Africa!

BEAUTY BASICS

When trying to build a beautiful zoo, keep your eye on the basics first. Each path section, each bit of fencing has its own special aesthetic impact on the zoo guests. Making the right choices there can save you a lot of trouble later. Of course, sometimes money will be too tight for you to buy what you'd prefer; when you're starting a new zoo and laying down paths, the $40 difference between a dirt path and a cobblestone path is a meaningful one.

In most scenarios, you'll find that it pays to put off beauty-related investments till later. If you design your zoo with foresight and leave extra space, adding beauty-enhancing items won't be a problem. For your purposes, these items fall roughly into two categories: items that can fit almost anywhere (for example, decorative lamps) and items that require dedicated space (for example, statues and fountains). It makes sense to postpone investing in the second class of items until the time comes to revise zoo layout. Revisions to

zoo layout automatically create lots of small areas (a few tiles apiece) that are perfect for placing larger zoo scenery objects. Of course, the requirements of a particular scenario may force you to make small exceptions to that rule.

In the later stages of any successful scenario, your zoo will be full of guests, and that's when unsightly trash becomes a problem. You must keep a vigilant eye on your maintenance workers—being very social types, they insist on traveling around in little bands (you know the score: one guy sweeps up the trash, the other five watch). In general, you'll find that you need about one maintenance worker for every 50 zoo guests and two zoo exhibits. That's just to keep your zoo reasonably trash-free; in times of emergency, such as when your exhibits are struck by a plague of deteriorating fencing, you may have to temporarily double the size of your maintenance staff.

TIP

When enough money does become available, think about replacing that dirt path before investing in foliage, fancy lamps, and care-intensive flowerbeds. Bulldozing the old path before laying down the new one will return most of your original expenditure, too, and offer an opportunity to improve traffic flow.

ZOO FINANCES

Now we come to the tycoon part of *Zoo Tycoon*: making money. As mentioned earlier, in *Zoo Tycoon* money does not make money. Money buys happiness, which in turn makes money.

You'll quickly see the infinite wisdom contained in that statement when you consider the sources of income available in the game. These are as follows:

- **Admission fees:** These are very important, accounting for most of your income throughout the early stages of zoo development (6 to 12 months). In the later stages of the game, admission fees tend to constitute around 40% of zoo income, providing you don't raise the price sharply in order to reduce the number of new guests. You may have to employ this tactic to restore order and happiness to your zoo: huge crowds mean dropping happiness. Watch out for this phenomenon when approaching the end of a scenario!

- **Concessions:** In *Zoo Tycoon*, concessions (guest amenities that charge a price for services) are the single most important source of income in the game. Concessions fall into two broad categories: those that sell items, and those that sell entertainment. It's always a good idea to invest in an animal theater and a carousel as soon as they're available (which is right away in many scenarios). Note that some attractions do not charge guests an admission price (for example, the petting zoo).

Nevertheless, the boost they give to guest happiness still makes them necessary additions to a growing zoo.

Donations: These tend to be the third most important source of income for your zoo (after concessions and admission fees) (see Figure 1.5). If your guests like what they see in your zoo, there's a chance they'll become zoo benefactors upon leaving. If you design your initial exhibits well and have very happy animals to show for it, you can count on winning several new benefactors a month, each of whom is good for several hundred dollars (most often between $500 and $700). You'll also receive big one-time donations if you succeed in reproducing an endangered species in your zoo, or if you win a particularly important award.

FIGURE 1.5:

Use the Zoo Status/Income and Expenses panel to keep track of zoo finances.

Recycling: This efficient-sounding category includes income derived from bulldozing (there are always buyers for that section of dirt path!), the sale of compost (you must build the appropriate facility first), and the sale of animals. As pointed out earlier, happy animals reproduce, and their zoo offspring reproduce further. Selling animals often causes fleeting unhappiness among fellow inmates, but the alternative—not selling any—means a gradual descent into gloom, doom, and insanity.

Remember: don't worry too much about money, worry about everyone being happy. You'll find lots more on the subject in Chapters 4 and 6.

TECHNICAL ISSUES

You may encounter performance problems, even though your machine meets the minimum specifications given on the game box, or even if it exceeds them slightly. This may occur even when you're playing at the default resolution of 800x600, and have already implemented all the performance–enhancing options listed in the game's ReadMe file. A big zoo with many guests can eat up all the RAM your computer has; the game will then slow down considerably while your box writes and reads data from the swap file. The quick, elegant solution is to install more RAM. Memory chips have become so cheap that the expense isn't a real consideration, and installing new RAM is a very simple procedure; ask your computer dealer to show you how on one of the mother-boards. A hundred bucks will buy at least half a gigabyte of RAM, which should fix *any* RAM problems. You won't regret that purchase.

Of course, it goes without saying that you keep your box in great shape, deleting truly unnecessary files with beady-eyed zeal and regularly running Windows' CleanUp Manager and Disk Defragmenter (or their equivalents, such as Norton Utilities). A computer that's well looked after will consistently outperform a significantly faster machine that has been neglected by its owner.

FACE TO FACE WITH THE INTERFACE

The game manual does a good job of explaining things, but there are a couple of extra things you should know. First of all, even though you've read the manual and played the tutorials, it's a good idea to quickly click through all the interface options. The number of choices available in certain menus may be slightly overwhelming, particularly in scenarios at the Intermediate and Advanced levels. Yet all these choices are important, and you should have a clear idea of what they mean before you jump into a game. You'll also notice a couple of quirks: the Fences button opens a menu that also includes decorative barriers, including a low green hedge that's extremely handy in improving zoo aesthetics—it can be placed virtually anywhere. Similarly, the Foliage menu contains many decorative foliage choices; scrolling down to the bottom of the foliage panel will reveal numerous flowerbeds, topiaries, etc. Exhibit structures such as animal shelters and animal toys are to be found in the Adopt Animals menu.

Finally, you'll become aware of a slight confusion when rotating the screen and/or objects with the help of the appropriate buttons. Here's what you should remember:

- **When rotating the screen,** the button on the left shows an arrow pointing right, but rotates the screen to the left. The button on the right shows an arrow pointing left, but it rotates the screen to the right. Left button rotates left, right button rotates right; ignore the arrows.

- **When rotating objects,** the button on the left shows an arrow pointing right and rotates objects to the right. The button on the right shows an arrow pointing left and rotates objects to the left. Follow the arrows; ignore the position of the buttons.

All clear? Good. It's time to roll up your sleeves and get down to the business of building a zoo, and that's where we'll pick up in the next chapter.

TIP

Open the Options menu and adjust Tool Tip duration to maximum while you're getting familiar with the game. You'll probably want to adjust it to minimum duration once you know more, as it tends to get in the way when you're laying down fencing and paths.

BUILDING YOUR ZOO

A VERY LARGE PART OF ZOO TYCOON'S GAMEPLAY CONSISTS OF PLANNING AND BUILDING YOUR ZOO. THE EARLIER, SHORTER SCENARIOS EMPHASIZE THIS ASPECT OF THE GAME VERY STRONGLY; ONE ("INNER CITY ZOO") MAKES GOOD ZOO DESIGN A WINNING CONDITION IN ITSELF. A POORLY DESIGNED ZOO DOES NOT NECESSARILY MEAN TOTAL DISASTER, AT LEAST AS LONG AS THE EXHIBITS MEET ANIMAL SPACE REQUIREMENTS AND THE HABITATS INSIDE MEET ANIMAL NEEDS. HOWEVER, A ZOO LIKE THAT WILL NEVER FULFILL EITHER YOUR HOPES OR ITS OWN POTENTIAL.

THIS CHAPTER IS MEANT TO ELIMINATE ALL YOUR DOUBTS, FEARS, AND DILEMMAS IN THE AREA OF ZOO DESIGN. IT BEGINS WITH A DISCUSSION OF GENERAL ZOO PLANNING CONCEPTS, FOLLOWED BY IMPORTANT PARTICULARS SUCH AS EXHIBIT DESIGN AND THE SIGNIFICANCE AND PLACING OF ZOO GUEST AMENITIES. ALL THESE ISSUES ARE EXAMINED WITH AN EYE TOWARD CONSTANT GROWTH, WHICH IS LIKELY TO BE YOUR PRIMARY GOAL. YOU'LL BE CONTINUOUSLY EXPANDING YOUR ZOO IN EVERY GAME YOU PLAY; THE END OF EXPANSION TENDS TO MEAN THE END OF THE GAME. KEEPING THIS IN MIND AT ALL TIMES WILL SAVE YOU LOTS OF TROUBLE.

THE PRACTICALITIES OF ZOO DESIGN

Let's make one thing clear at the outset: *Zoo Tycoon* is a computer game, and computer games exist to let you do whatever you like. It is not the purpose of this book to force solutions down your throat—there's enough of that going on in so-called real life. The zoo concepts discussed in this section aren't the only feasible approaches to playing the game; they are simply solid, viable concepts intended to help players who want to do well and are uncertain how to go about it. *Zoo Tycoon* is a forgiving game, and you should always feel free to experiment with whatever approach strikes your fancy.

Many scenarios feature partially built zoos, and freeform maps always include pre-laid paths. Do not be led blindly into basing your zoo concept on what's already there (see Figure 2.1). In fact, most often the best solution is to bulldoze everything, thus adding a nice wad of cash to your starting money. The following sections assume that you did so, and that you're starting your design from scratch.

FIGURE 2.1:

It's often better to bulldoze everything and start anew; the Burkitsville Zoo scenario proves the point.

First Steps

Your first step should always be a review of available adoption options followed by a review of zoo-building options and a quick check of available cash. Specific scenario conditions will impose particular design requirements, while freeform games initially feature very few buildings and zoo animals (see Chapter 8), and only two kinds of paths (dirt and concrete). Once you have an idea of what's feasible, begin by building paths, not exhibits or buildings.

Your network of paths will determine your zoo layout, so you should proceed thoughtfully. Of course, if you like games such as *Dungeon Keeper*, it may amuse you to build a zoo featuring a lonely washroom at the end of a long, winding path lined with numerous attractions and food/drink stands (no restaurants!). However, this kind of layout will make for poor traffic flow, which is bad.

> ## TIP
>
> *Use the CTRL+G command to turn grid overlay on and off while you're planning and building your zoo. The grid makes calculating exhibit size and placing everything in the right spot much easier!*

Understanding Zoo Traffic

All good path networks share one important quality: They ensure smooth traffic flow. Crowding becomes a concern as soon as the number of guests reaches three figures, and may ruin all your other fine efforts to improve the overall guest happiness level (as indicated by the Guest Happiness bar near the lower-left corner of the main game screen). Guest crowding defines your zoo's maximum guest capacity: It may force you to hike the admission price way, way up in order to discourage more guests from entering your zoo. Of course, that's bad news for a tycoon, since it means a loss of potential revenue.

The simplest way to prevent traffic jams is to make sure every part of your zoo can be reached by multiple routes, and that the paths in your zoo are wide enough. Single-lane paths simply don't do the job once your zoo reaches a certain size. A freeform game played on a large map may necessitate

> ## NOTE
>
> *If you think of your zoo as a living organism, then zoo guests are its lifeblood, rich in nutrients (dollars, dollars!). Your zoo layout should encourage them to circulate everywhere, spreading largesse along the way.*

triple-lane paths! Regardless of the path/zoo layout you choose, build big path junctions. Let intersecting paths form a square that features seating for tired guests, a basic set of guest amenities (food/drink/restroom), and selected decorative objects.

Major intersections provide an opportunity to build big plazas lined with concessions and attractions. Such plazas tend to act like big people magnets, and you should make sure you balance traffic flow by placing highly attractive exhibits on each arm of every major intersection. Put these exhibits some distance away from the intersections; if they're right next to the plaza/ amenities area, they will increase crowding instead of decreasing it.

In order to understand zoo traffic flow, it helps to realize that the guests entering your zoo fall into three categories:

🐾 **Free agents:** These guests choose directions to walk in at random. You can exercise some influence on their movements by making sure each part of your zoo can be reached by several different routes. This maximizes the chance that a carefree wanderer will explore your whole zoo, spending lots of money in the process.

🐾 **People with a need:** Guests who are hungry, thirsty, tired, etc. will be looking for the closest "satisfier" of their need. If the nearest food/drink stand, bench, etc. is too crowded, they'll keep looking to satisfy their need, choosing the next closest "satisfier" and so on. Putting guest amenities on or near intersections helps traffic flow nicely.

🐾 **People with a purpose:** These folks know what they want and always walk in the direction of what they perceive as the biggest attraction. The influence of an attraction is modified by its distance from the guest in question: A smaller attraction nearby may have bigger pull than a big attraction some distance away (note that in this context, "attractions" include animal exhibits as well as buildings, such as the animal theater, carousel, etc.). By placing attractions and amenities thoughtfully, you can make your guests follow a route that has been more or less predetermined by you.

Now that you know how traffic flows in *Zoo Tycoon*, let's examine a couple of viable zoo concepts.

Zoo Concepts

All zoo layouts are of necessity at least partly defined by the shape of the exhibits, which tend to be rectangular. In addition, paths can only run straight or turn at right angles; inevitably, the most efficient zoo layouts tend to be variations on the grid concept. You'll find that the grid approach makes zoo planning very easy as long as you don't fall into the trap of trying to space everything evenly.

However, in order to throw you a little curve and get you thinking outside the grid, we'll first take a look at a different zoo layout concept. This is the layout featured in the pre-built zoo in the very first game scenario ("Small Zoo"). It features single exhibits laid out on both sides of the path.

The Leaf

This layout resembles a many-bladed leaf. It features a main, central path, preferably wide (leaf stem), with side paths leading to individual exhibits (leaf blades—see Figure 2.2). The Leaf layout has several important advantages:

- The side paths act as traffic decongestants, siphoning guests off the central path whenever they choose to view a particular exhibit.

- The relatively large, landscaped observation areas in this layout make zoo guests stay for quite a while, bombarding them with positive aesthetic input and simultaneously increasing hunger/thirst.

- Guests are less likely to make animals feel crowded. The length of the connecting path can act as an auxiliary filter; the longer it is, the less likely it is that guests will walk all the way to the exhibit. However, longer connecting paths almost invariably cause some wasted space.

- Designing a zoo based on this approach is very easy. All you have to do is lay down the central path, then add exhibits and connecting paths as necessary.

When creating zoos based on this layout, build a cross-shaped junction every four to six exhibits. The center of that junction should consist of a square or a plaza replete with guest amenities and decorative objects (fountains, sculptures, etc.). The side paths leading off the first junction become new main paths, with connecting paths to exhibits on either side, and so on.

Jan, Year 1 $75,000

FIGURE 2.2:
The "Small Zoo" scenario features a slightly stunted Leaf layout; note that ending the main path with an exhibit observation area makes expansion difficult.

You should plan subsequent junctions so that all the main paths end up forming squares. The interior of each square should be filled with exhibits and their observation areas. You'll run into the greatest drawback of this zoo layout there and then, for it is very difficult to lay out a zoo this way without wasting some space.

Ideally, the exhibits between the junctions should form a theme area where exhibits feature animals from the same habitat, such as savannah or rainforest creatures. In practice you may have to bend this rule, as the number of species per type of habitat varies greatly. When faced with a gap on one side of the main central path, consider putting one of the zoo attractions there (such as a carousel, petting zoo, etc.).

THE GRID

This zoo layout involves running paths around individual big exhibits or groups of smaller exhibits; if you leave space between the exhibit and the path, it is very easy to widen the path later, add an observation area, and insert benches or decorative objects. This approach has several important advantages:

- **Ease of execution:** There's nothing simpler than laying down a bit of path, building an exhibit alongside it (but at least one row of tiles away!), then arranging the path to complete a rectangle around the exhibit. If you want to group several exhibits inside this rectangle, simply build one very large exhibit that covers most of the rectangle's area, then divide it up with extra barriers (for instance, split it in half). Creating new exhibits this way lets you save quite a few bucks in fencing costs.

Exhibits that utilize the outer zoo wall as one of exhibit barriers can be considerably less expensive to build. This is particularly convenient when you're starting a freeform game with little money.

- **Flexibility:** The Grid layout makes rearranging and expanding your zoo very easy. It's completely consistent with the notion of tiled terrain; all calculations involving space are greatly simplified.

- **Easy guest access to every part of the zoo:** With the Grid layout, a guest who walks a single block is almost literally swallowed up by your zoo, spending a record amount of time and money inside. This is because every single intersection of the Grid opens up multiple routes to numerous exhibits and attractions; your guest is constantly, mercilessly pulled along the path.

The first thing to do when building a Grid-type zoo is to lay down the entrance crossroads. The crossroads should always be located five to six tiles away from the zoo entrance (see Figure 2.3). This will let you comfortably fit quite a few things next to the outer zoo wall.

FIGURE 2.3:

A few hundred bucks saved on fencing right at the start of a game can mean as much as ten thousand later on. Note the triple-lane path by the zoo entrance.

THE FORK

This is a variation on the Grid approach. It works especially well for laying out zoos that can accommodate 500 or more guests at a time (the type of zoo you'll need in later scenarios and large-map freeform games). This zoo layout is called the Fork because the main paths feature a lane divider from two to five tiles wide (see Figure 2.4). The divider space is subsequently used to place guest amenities and decorative objects, or simply to lay down connecting paths between the two lanes, which reduces traffic congestion.

FIGURE 2.4:

The Fork layout requires advance planning—think things out before you lay down a single path tile.

The Fork offers supreme flexibility: Single-lane paths can be widened at any time, thanks to the divider. The ease with which you can place guest amenities is a big advantage when you're trying to keep hundreds of zoo guests fed, watered, and, um, relieved. This is particularly important in scenarios where you're required to achieve a very high level of guest happiness; a couple of unhappy zoo guests who don't feel like walking may cause you to lose the game. If need be, you can avoid this sad outcome by plonking down the appropriate zoo building (food stand, drink stand, or washroom) right in front of their lazy faces. Of course, you should only undertake such drastic action when the scenario time limit draws near.

CREATING OBSERVATION AREAS

As a rule, you should make sure that there are two tiles of space between the path and the exhibit fence. This lets you insert an observation area right next to the path simply by laying down a short stretch of pathway alongside (see Figure 2.5). Guests cannot view an exhibit from a distance of three tiles; they'll walk all the way round the exhibit to the observation area, and then they'll have to walk all the way back again. This reduces crowding and results in more food and drink sales.

TIP

Guests have a "sight range" of 10 tiles. Keep this in mind when building exhibits and observation areas. Extra large exhibits containing numerous animals should have observation areas on all sides.

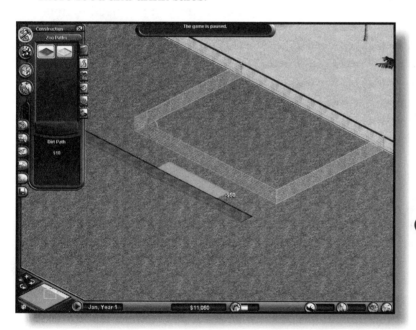

FIGURE 2.5:

This is the most efficient way to mark out an observation area.

Observation areas perform several functions. Their size helps define the number of guests who can view the exhibit at any one time, thus reducing the risk of unhappiness among shy animals. They also have a positive effect on zoo beauty.

CREATING EXHIBITS

The first thing to keep in mind when building a new exhibit is this: Size matters. There is a point, however, beyond which an increase in size brings no further benefits; let's call it maximum exhibit size. This size is defined by the exhibit's maximum attractiveness, for you cannot increase exhibit attractiveness indefinitely (the attractiveness of specific exhibits is discussed in detail in Chapter 3; every animal description has a relevant entry).

CALCULATING EXHIBIT SIZE

Calculating the minimum exhibit size is easy. Every animal has its own space requirements and social needs: you just need to multiply an animal's personal space requirement by the number of animals in the exhibit. However, building tiny exhibits like that only makes sense in the first couple of scenarios.

As a rule, bigger exhibits are better exhibits. They can contain more animals, and each animal increases the attractiveness of the exhibit. They provide an opportunity to place more happiness-boosting foliage and rocks. They also allow trouble-free reproduction among the animals within the exhibit.

Calculating maximum *sensible* exhibit size isn't that easy, and varies widely from game to game. It obviously depends on the size of the zoo and the amount of species you want this zoo to have, which in turn determines the number of exhibits. A scenario such as "Inner City Zoo" may force you to squeeze four African savannah species into the minimum allowable space; the same exhibit should be several times bigger in a large-map freeform game.

Generally, you'll want exhibits big enough to accommodate the maximum allowable number of adult animals (see Chapter 3). Most games will force you to scale back from this ideal; but you should always make an exhibit big enough to accommodate a *family* of animals, even when the animals involved don't need any companions to stay happy.

Please note that creating a habitat inside an exhibit is discussed in Chapter 3.

TIP

Each baby animal has the same space requirements as an adult. However, baby animals do not count toward the maximum allowable number of animals within an exhibit; only adults do. For example, an exhibit containing two adult and one baby rhino will not be penalized for animal crowding, even though two is the maximum number of rhinos allowed in a single exhibit.

Everything You've Ever Wanted to Know About Exhibit Barriers

Upon opening up the Construction menu, Fences tab, you'll immediately see that there are two kinds of barriers or fences:

> **TIP**
>
> Remember the zoo guests' sight range when building exhibits! The maximum practical distance between observation areas on opposite sides of the exhibit fence is 20 tiles.

☞ **Decorative fences:** These cannot be used to create exhibits, but they fulfill a very useful role in making your zoo more beautiful (see Chapter 6 for details).

☞ **Exhibit barriers:** These are the barriers we'll be focusing on in this section. They come in two basic varieties: full height and low.

Most animals are capable of jumping over the lower barriers, so they won't work if you're attempting to confine anything other than a low-slung quadruped (like the saltwater crocodile or warthog). This is unfortunate because low fencing has a couple of advantages. It always allows zoo guests to look inside the exhibit, regardless of the material it's made from; and of course it's considerably less expensive than the full-height variety.

> **TIP**
>
> Low-height fencing can also be used in combination with another barrier (for example, a moat around a low fence, or sinking an exhibit a few levels into the ground). Animals can't jump over low fencing if another barrier is present outside.

Full-height barriers can confine all animals except primates within their exhibits (including the flamingo). Primates can climb over some of the full-height fencing types; the game provides relevant info when you select a fence type. Guests cannot see into an exhibit through full-height solid fencing such as the concrete wall, but that's not necessarily a disadvantage. It's actually very helpful in building exhibits for animals that feel uncomfortable when viewed by a large number of guests. Several scenarios require you to successfully breed shy, inhibited animals such as the okapi; placing a species like that in an exhibit with see-through barriers on all four sides means almost certain failure (see Chapter 3 for more details).

The vast majority of your exhibits will utilize full-height barriers, most commonly a mixture of solid and see-through fencing types (see Figure 2.6). Other than that, the effectiveness of these barriers is based on their strength and durability.

Jun, Year 2 $7,315

FIGURE 2.6:

A concrete wall is, predictably, the best way to ensure some privacy.

Barrier Strength and Age *Zoo Tycoon* features a staggering array of fencing, from assorted rustic wooden types (models with or without windows are available), to classic iron bars and modern-looking plexiglas walls; to the prison-like concrete wall topped by chain-link fencing. Each of these types of fencing is assigned a strength rating; the ratings range from 200 (chain link) to 300 (full concrete). As game time passes, the fences gradually decay, moving into a state of deterioration (indicated by a yellow fencing symbol on the exhibit list, as explained in the game manual) and subsequently into nonexistence (indicated by red fencing on the exhibit list). Weak fencing decays faster; a chain-link fence can deteriorate in the space of just six months (you'll see this process in the main game screen).

Once a fence is officially classified as deteriorated, there is a possibility that the contained animal will break out of the exhibit, causing panic and a sharp drop in the happiness of zoo guests. Don't worry, no one ever gets hurt; as a matter of fact, the screams are highly entertaining. The runaway beast invariably gets cornered by a zookeeper and put away in a container, so you might as well let a fence deteriorate when it's safe (i.e., when there's no scenario deadline approaching) and treat yourself to a little extra action.

NOTE

Freeform games begin with a very limited choice of structures, path types, foliage, and animal species. New choices become available every three months, so be patient.

There are two things you can do to avoid unwanted problems with exhibit barriers:

- **Build strong barriers**: This eliminates the need to frequently check the exhibit list. Wood-slat and stickpole fencing has a surprisingly slow deterioration rate, but it still won't outlast iron bars.

- **Hire plenty of maintenance workers:** Although you can replace damaged segments of fencing yourself, this costs as much as buying a new section. Having plenty of maintenance workers is desirable anyway (see Chapter 4).

Do not let barrier cost determine the size of your new exhibit. If you don't have enough money to build the barrier for the exhibit you want, wait a little.

> ### NOTE
>
> *Not all animal species are capable of breaking through deteriorated fencing, and those that are have varying strength. Predictably, an elephant will be quicker to break down decayed barriers than a wildebeest, and an ostrich will stay put within its exhibit until the fence crumbles into dust.*

Zoo Structures

Zoo Tycoon features a breathtaking range of structures, from elephant rides to compost buildings. Some make you money and some don't; not all are strictly necessary in a great zoo. And as you would expect, some are more important than others.

This section discusses the types of structures available and their respective roles in the success of your zoo. It does not discuss decorative objects or view things from an aesthetic angle (see Chapter 6), nor does it explore the deeper financial aspects of running profitable zoo concessions (see Chapter 7).

> ### NOTE
>
> *When playing a new freeform game on the Hard level, you may have no choice but to build chain-link fencing to start with. Treat exhibits with such fencing as temporary, to be rebuilt later when you have more money and more fencing types to choose from. Animal houses are discussed in Chapters 3, 5, and 6.*

Placing Structures

Naturally, no structure should be plopped down at random. As mentioned earlier in this chapter, path intersections are good sites for concessions, attractions, and conveniences. (Keep in mind that the zoo entrance ranks as a major intersection even if you've neglected to build a crossroads nearby as recommended earlier.) You should know that new guests entering the zoo have random hunger/thirst/energy levels; some may need a bite, a drink, and a seat right away.

The siting of certain guest conveniences—benches, vending machines, and restrooms—shouldn't be restricted to the areas around path intersections. Guest conveniences are often needed in miscellaneous spots; if you've laid out your zoo leaving small areas of free space as recommended throughout this book, you'll find additions like these very easy.

The structures discussed below are organized according to the role they play in a zoo. Note that Appendices B and C contain numerical data pertaining to structure cost, capacity, aesthetic impact, and effect on guest happiness (for example, adults are predictably happy when they see a restaurant).

CONVENIENCES

This category includes restrooms, trashcans, benches and picnic tables, and vending machines.

Vending machines can service one person at a time and are classified as concessions in the game (they carry an upkeep cost of $10 a month). However, they're simply too small in every respect to be regarded as anything but conveniences. The profits derived from the sale of candy and soda are insignificant, and the resulting effect on guest hunger/thirst is slight; however, the vending machines' small footprint makes it easy to fit them almost anywhere, even though they always have to be accompanied by a trashcan. As explained in the manual, food/drink consumption results in trash, and your conscientious zoo guests like to be able to place trash in the appropriate receptacle (in addition to putting a premium on a trash-free zoo).

Benches allow zoo guests to rest (regain energy); **picnic tables** allow them to rest and eat. You should place benches and picnic tables on the tile next to the path, not the path itself. It pays to arrange rest areas featuring decorative objects (see Chapter 6). It's both smart and almost always possible to fit in a small rest area *behind* the food/drink stands that necessitate its existence (see Figure 2.7); guests who just bought food should be drawn away from the path in their search for a seat, not right back into the traffic.

Zoo Tycoon features two types of **restrooms**. The family restroom is infinitely preferable to the basic model (which you'll be stuck with the first few months of a freeform game). It can service eight guests at a time instead of two, which is quite heroic.

TIP

Begin building a new zoo some distance away from the zoo entrance. Space by the zoo entrance becomes increasingly valuable as the game goes on; it's invariably the most valuable piece of real estate in really big zoos.

The game is paused.

Nov. Year 3

FIGURE 2.7:

Placing a rest area behind the food stands saves space and improves traffic flow.

FOOD AND DRINK STANDS

If there's one outstanding, dominating trait shared by all of your zoo guests, it is this: They like to eat. Boy, do they like to eat. After they've eaten, they like to drink, and after they've drank they like to go brush their teeth, as recommended by all dentists. Remembering this sequence will help you place food and drink stands with precision after considering the traffic flow.

Food and drink stands are not available at the start of a freeform game. This does not make much difference, as a couple of vending machines will satisfy your initial guests' needs (this might not

TIP

Vending machines work well as emergency hunger/thirst quenchers even when placed in relatively remote locations. Their low upkeep cost compensates for the low profit potential. Once your zoo has grown to a certain size, try placing a combination of candy/soda machines on paths leading to restrooms; you'll be surprised how many guests need a drink/bite after doing business. Setting up a couple of benches by the restroom path is also a very good idea!

be true if you're an ace playing at the Easy level and convert the starting money into a multitude of exhibits while setting the admission price very low). All food and drink stands are classified as concessions; their upkeep costs $50 a month. It's a very good idea to place one or more trashcans nearby!

The first food stand to make an appearance in a freeform game is the **hot dog stand**. It can service two guests at a time, which isn't a big improvement over the vending machine—especially since a stand takes up two times more space. However, consuming a hot dog decreases a guest's hunger meaningfully; it also significantly increases the guest's thirst. For this reason, a hot dog stand should ideally be accompanied by a **drink stand**. Stand-alone drink stands do not do well in any but the busiest zoos; their capacity to handle four customers at a time is a little misleading in that respect.

The **burger shack** is the first food concession to have really good profit potential, partly because it can serve three guests at a time. It is a pleasant sight for every adult, hungry or not. While a burger is twice as filling as a hot dog, it stimulates thirst to a lesser degree. A burger shack takes up twice as much space as a hot dog stand, and the increased customer traffic makes a nearby rest area absolutely necessary.

The **ice cream stand** is especially popular with children, but adults like it too; it is one of the best overall food concession choices in the game even though it serves just two customers at a time. It makes little difference in guest hunger (on par with vending machine candy) and, interestingly, increases thirst like a burger. The sharp-eyed tycoon will recognize the consequent potential for many repeat visits, as well as for improved beverage sales. Being of pleasant appearance, ice cream stands make good additions to rest areas landscaped for positive aesthetic impact.

The **pizza shack** is the most efficient food-serving establishment in this group. As the game points out, due to pizza's circular nature, it can be sliced and sold to as many as six customers at a time. This underscores the need for a decent-sized rest area nearby, as well as an extra trashcan or two, especially since pizza increases guest thirst as sharply as a hot dog. Alert tycoons should not get overly excited by the possibility of building hot dog stand/pizza shack combos with a couple of drink stands nearby. Pizza is very filling, and a guest who has partaken of some won't be ready for another meal for quite some time. Two or even three hot dog stands work much harder at generating business for your drink stands.

NOTE

Remember that food and drink sales are also influenced by the price you set. Naturally, lower prices result in bigger sales and higher guest happiness; see Chapter 7 for more details.

RESTAURANTS

Restaurants belong in a category of their own. They provide a complete package of guest services, including varied food choices (pizza, hot dog, and burger) as well as drinks, a place to rest, a place to dispose of trash, and a restroom. The restaurants in *Zoo Tycoon* can serve 12 guests at a time; they are the unequaled moneymakers in the game's catering business, so don't be deterred by the higher purchase and upkeep cost ($500 per month). You'll have to wait a while before the restaurant becomes an option in a freeform game; however, once it does, it's an entirely sound idea to switch over the entire food concession business to restaurants and ice cream stands only (supplemented by convenient soda and candy machines).

Adults love the sight of a restaurant, to say nothing of the joy they feel at its very existence. However, children are understandably neutral (stop fidgeting, take your hands out from under the table, be quiet, etc.). This is why they'll really appreciate seeing an ice cream stand nearby—it holds out the promise of better times.

ATTRACTIONS

Zoo Tycoon offers you the opportunity to build five types of zoo attractions: petting zoo, Japanese garden, elephant ride, carousel, and animal theater. All have a positive effect on guest happiness and zoo rating, and the last two attractions are terrific moneymakers!

As a rule, attractions are best placed either as part of a junction/plaza complex or singly in strategic spots where they'll exert a positive influence on traffic flow. It is important to position the entrance to an attraction carefully; making access difficult may result in horrific traffic jams.

The **petting zoo** is free of charge. Understandably more popular with children, it nevertheless has a tonic effect on the family as a whole. However, because it takes up a considerable amount of space and can accommodate only four guests at a time, it is not a high-priority attraction; it's probably best considered in the middle stages of the game, well after it becomes available. Petting zoos don't incur upkeep costs.

The **Japanese garden** is a favorite with adults; children like it, too. It scores remarkably high on the aesthetics chart, but again can only accommodate four guests at a time. Nevertheless, the numerous benefits conferred by this attraction make it a good choice as soon as it becomes available and affordable, even though admission is free. A really big, successful zoo usually has several Japanese gardens; they do not incur upkeep costs.

The **elephant ride**, being able to accommodate just two guests at a time, offers miserly profits (upkeep cost is $50 a month). It's popular with children and somewhat less so with adults, who as the game warns you dislike the smell. This is not a high-priority attraction, although of course eventually you'll build it just to increase your zoo's rating and improve guest happiness.

The **carousel** is a terrific choice as soon as it becomes available and at any later stage in zoo development. A big, successful zoo has several carousels; big freeform maps easily allow up to six or seven. Carousels are very popular with zoo guests and very profitable even if you sharply cut the ride price; they can accommodate 12 guests at a time. Carousels are great favorites with children! Upkeep costs $100 a month.

The **animal theater** (see Figure 2.8) is the biggest zoo attraction in terms of size and profit potential (monthly upkeep is $50). Shows are staged for up to 12 guests at a time, and have a positive if unspectacular effect on the whole family. This is a high-priority attraction that you should always acquire as soon as it becomes available. A successful zoo has several animal theaters, all of them doing brisk business.

FIGURE 2.8:

Building an animal theater marks a new stage in the development of your zoo.

THE COMPOST BUILDING

This is yet another building in a category of its own (in several senses). The compost building will bring respectable if unspectacular profits ($50 per every pile of poo raked up by the zookeeper) without incurring upkeep costs; however, its smelly presence is unpleasant for zoo guests. It does not require an access path or maintenance, and so it can be safely tucked away in the farthest corner of your zoo. However, once your zoo runs out of space, you should consider getting rid of it.

GIFT STANDS AND GIFT SHOPS

A gift stand is more of a convenience than a moneymaking concession. Its profits are too small to be of any significance until the number of guests in your zoo hits three figures; and once your zoo grows to this size, it's time to consider building the larger gift shop, which automatically reduces gift stands to convenience status. However, though gift stands won't improve your profits much, they do affect guest happiness; people enjoy being able to buy a souvenir from the zoo—as evidenced by their thoughts in the guest info panel. The gift stand's small footprint will let you fit it almost anywhere you want without trouble; a good spot in the early game is just by the entrance. Other natural sites for gift stands and shops include the squares and plazas marking path intersections.

Gift stands can serve just one customer at a time; gift shops can accommodate 12. Monthly upkeep costs are $50 and $200, respectively.

THE ZOO ANIMALS

AS AN ENTERPRISING ZOO TYCOON, YOU MUST ALWAYS REMEMBER THAT A ZOO IS BASICALLY AN ENTERTAINMENT COMPLEX. NOW, EVERY ENTERTAINMENT HAS ITS STARS, AND IN A ZOO, THE ANIMALS ARE THE STARS OF THE SHOW.

ZOO TYCOON FEATURES ANIMALS BELONGING TO 47 DIFFERENT SPECIES. MANY OF THESE ARE NOT AVAILABLE RIGHT AWAY; FOR EXAMPLE, YOU'LL HAVE TO INVEST PLENTY OF MONEY AND PATIENCE BEFORE THE GIANT PANDA BECOMES ATTAINABLE AS AN EXHIBIT OPTION (SEE CHAPTER 5 FOR DETAILS). TWO EXTRA MYSTERY BEASTS BECOME AVAILABLE ONLY AFTER YOU'VE COMPLETED THE FINAL TWO SCENARIOS. HOWEVER, EVEN THE SOMEWHAT LIMITED CHOICES POSSIBLE AT THE START OF A SCENARIO ARE NUMEROUS ENOUGH TO CONFUSE AN ASPIRING TYCOON.

THIS CHAPTER IS DESIGNED TO ELIMINATE CONFUSION AND DOUBT FROM ALL YOUR DEALINGS WITH THE ZOO ANIMALS. IT OPENS WITH A DISCUSSION OF OUTSTANDING ANIMAL ISSUES, SO TO SPEAK. THESE ARE THE CONSIDERATIONS INVOLVED IN PURCHASING AN ANIMAL AND CARING FOR IT THEREAFTER. THE LATER, BIGGER PART OF THIS CHAPTER TAKES A LOOK AT EVERY ANIMAL THAT APPEARS IN ZOO TYCOON. EACH ENTRY EXAMINES THE ANIMAL'S REQUIREMENTS AND CHARACTERISTICS, AND SHOULD HELP YOU MAKE AN INFORMED DECISION WHEN EXPANDING YOUR ZOO. NOTE THAT EXHIBITS ARE ALSO DISCUSSED IN CHAPTER 2, AND THAT THE APPENDICES AT THE END OF THIS BOOK CONTAIN USEFUL DATA ABOUT THE GAME'S ANIMALS.

ACQUIRING ANIMALS

It's time for some serious tycoon money talk! Now, the first thing you have to remember is this: animals cost much more than their purchase price. In fact, the dollars you pay to adopt an animal constitute a small fraction of the real cost. This is because the real cost includes building an appropriate exhibit, which (as explained in Chapter 2) can get very expensive.

To illustrate the thought process and the money involved in adopting a new animal, here's a practical example. Let's say you're starting a freeform game and are looking for something inexpensive to kick things off. A look at the dollar numbers on the Adopt Animal menu will tell you that a Thomson's gazelle is the cheapest choice, simply unbeatable at just $500 (see Figure 3.1). However, like many herbivores it's a herd animal, so it requires a companion (preferably more than one), which instantly multiplies the purchase price. What's more, you'll have to build a larger exhibit, since every animal requires a certain amount of personal space to remain happy. It's obvious right away that a Thomson's gazelle is not the right choice when starting a new zoo with little money. And once you've read the rest of this chapter, you'll also know that this animal isn't very hot in terms of attractiveness (meaning an animal's ability to attract zoo guests, not its actual looks).

It's worth noting, however, that if you're starting a new zoo with a lot of cash, the Thomson's gazelle is a good choice. As a savannah herbivore, it likes the presence of other animal species and isn't very exacting about its habitat (meaning it will stay happy at a relatively low level of habitat suitability, indicated by the bottom bar in the Animal Information panel). It's very easy to build a large exhibit dedicated to animals of the African savannah that includes four different easygoing species. An exhibit like that is pretty cost-effective in terms of cash spent per species exhibited and rates highly with zoo guests, who rightly like evidence of thoughtfulness and good planning on your part.

The golden rule is this: when buying animals don't think just in terms of animals; think in terms of exhibits. This way of thinking will allow you to quickly calculate the real cost of acquiring a new species for your zoo. What's more, it will help you to always view your zoo as an entity. In this entity, exhibits are components of theme areas arranged for maximum guest happiness and thus maximum spending (both Chapter 6 and real life demonstrate that happiness and spending money go together).

TIP

Quite a few animal species are social types that require companions to stay happy, and others require hilly habitats that call for expensive adjustments to terrain elevation. Make sure you're aware of the hidden costs! The in-game Animal Information panel provides plenty of useful info that isn't repeated in this book.

To account for indirect costs, you should mentally multiply any adoption price by at least ten.

ANIMAL ATTRACTION

No, it's not quite what you think. In *Zoo Tycoon*, animal attraction or attractiveness is the pull an animal has with zoo guests. More people want to see a lion than an anteater, which is not surprising. Naturally, rare animals command extra attention, and baby animals are invariably a great hit. A baby animal is always three times more attractive than an adult animal, regardless of species. The efficient tycoon takes full advantage of this business opportunity and arranges things appropriately (see the next section).

The individual animal descriptions later on in this chapter always include a comment on the animal's attractiveness. You'll quickly see that enormous differences are involved! However, also keep in mind that five animals belonging to a relatively unexciting species can constitute a bigger attraction than a lonely exotic specimen—especially if there are baby animals in the group.

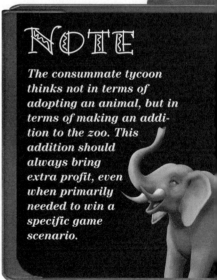

NOTE

The consummate tycoon thinks not in terms of adopting an animal, but in terms of making an addition to the zoo. This addition should always bring extra profit, even when primarily needed to win a specific game scenario.

An animal's attractiveness is especially important in a freeform game, where you start a zoo from scratch (Chapter 8 explains how to succeed even with next to no starting money). Scenario goals make attractiveness a secondary consideration; naturally, you'll still want to place the exhibits with the more attractive animals in strategic spots, ensuring good traffic flow with plenty of money being spent along the way.

WARNING

Deciding which animal to sell isn't easy. Reason dictates that you should sell the oldest animals first (they all have a limited life span). You should always check the sex of the animal you intend to sell (heart icon on the animal information panel) and make sure you leave a male–female pair to ensure continued reproduction within the exhibit. Also, it usually doesn't make sense to sell baby animals; they don't count towards an exhibit's population total, but still count in terms of attractiveness.

REPRODUCTION

According to some, reproduction constitutes the meaning of life, and you should certainly make it your #1 goal while playing *Zoo Tycoon* (animal reproduction, that is, not your own).

This is so for several weighty reasons. To begin with, as mentioned in Chapter 1, reproduction is the ultimate approval your animals can give to their habitats. Every animal has to reach a certain threshold of happiness in order to consider starting a family; animals are very nice and normal in this respect. This threshold can vary—see the next section.

Having your animals reproduce also means a big boost to the attractiveness of the given exhibit. For example, an adult anteater has an attractiveness of 10, so a pair—male and female—give the exhibit an attractiveness of 20. Now, a baby anteater, like all baby animals, is three times more attractive than an adult—this gives us a value of 30. It follows that the appearance of a baby anteater more than doubles the attractiveness of that particular exhibit!

Reproduction is not instantaneous; you'll have to wait a while before babies bounce onto the scene. What's more, every baby animal eventually turns into an adult, and these grown-up animals can reproduce, too. This is nice, since every extra animal boosts the attractiveness of the exhibit. However, sooner or later the babies grow up, the adult animals become too crowded, and it becomes absolutely necessary to sell some.

Note that if you sell one of a pair, the remaining animal's happiness is sharply affected. Also, selling a baby or one of a group of highly social animals (for example, a herd animal or a monkey) will affect the happiness of every animal in the exhibit. However, if you've created the right habitat things will soon bounce back to normal.

How Does It Happen?

Zoo Tycoon deals with this thorny question in a simple and logical manner. To start with, as you're aware by now, an animal has to be very happy in its habitat. The minimum happiness required is 85%, 90% is common, and some species require a happiness of 99% (as explained in Chapter 6, you'll always want all animals 100% happy anyway). Naturally, the animal you want to reproduce must have a mate.

Every now and then, the game runs what might be called a "fertility" check. If the previously discussed conditions are met, this is followed by a "fertility" roll; the probabilities involved range from 1% to 3%, depending on the species. As you can see, the chance of an animal becoming pregnant is pretty small; however, the game runs several checks a year, and sooner or later animals whose happiness/habitat requirements are met will reproduce. The number of offspring will be either one or two, depending on the species. Researching Animal Fertility (Animal Care, Research Program) increases the reproduction chance.

The Adoption Plan

So now you know that there's more to acquiring an animal than meeting the sticker price. The following steps outline how you should proceed once you've made up your mind to adopt one. Some scenarios may require a different approach (see Chapter 8 for details), but as a general rule you'll do well when following this procedure.

1   Check your cash *twice*. You need about 10 times as much as the animal's purchase price to afford an exhibit of generous size.

2   Know what you're getting into. When you select an animal, you'll see panels showing its preferred terrain type and preferred foliage type (note the icons at the bottom of the Adopt Animals menu). Next, click the Animal Facts button (marked with an "i" for "information") to read up on the selected animal. Pay particular attention to any facts relevant to the animal's preferred habitat and sociability. Animals that like the companionship of other animals, hilly or mountainous terrain, or thick vegetation are always more expensive regardless of the posted price.

3   Create the exhibit for your new animal before you actually complete the purchase. Don't create the entire habitat at this point; just place the chosen type of fencing, name the exhibit, and assign a zookeeper to it.

You'll need a bigger exhibit if you're buying more than one animal! Pause the game at this point; give careful consideration to where you place the exhibit gate—you should minimize distances between gates, and place them so as to mark out a route for the zookeeper(s). You may want to complete adjustments to paths, place aesthetic objects (exhibit info sign!), and build desired guest attractions/amenities before you finish working on the exhibit. Make sure the exhibit gate is not blocked!

4 Buy your chosen beast and place it inside the new exhibit. Open the Animal Information panel, then click "zookeeper recommendations" within the panel. This will give you a fairly precise idea of your new animal's habitat preferences. It's a good idea to place a few tiles of the animal's preferred terrain type before you unpause the game, or it might get unhappy before you finish building the exhibit with the game running.

5 If you want to continue building the exhibit with the game still paused, you won't get the happy/sad faces that indicate animal approval/disapproval of your actions. However, you can still get good feedback by clicking zookeeper recommendations on and off (they have to be clicked off in order to be updated). It's a little troublesome, though, because if you place more than a couple of tiles, trees, bushes, or rocks at a time, you might go too far.

6 Name your animal according to its sex. This will allow you to instantly tell whether it's a male or a female without rooting around in the animal info panel and is a neat way of establishing family relationships. Note that the oldest animal always appears on top of the exhibit list (click exhibit gate, then panda icon in the exhibit information panel); you don't need to rely on default names such as Lion 1, Lion 2, and Lion 3 to have an indication of an animal's age.

NOTE

It's virtually impossible to get the habitat inside the exhibit 100% right when the game is paused. Getting the final few percent right usually involves watching like a hawk for sad/happy faces while juggling selected rocks, foliage, and individual terrain tiles. Be prepared to lose some money on multiple little changes—perfection ain't cheap.

Of course, there's another, simpler way of getting things right. This involves playing the game with this book cracked open in your lap and referring to the appropriate animal description/appendix as necessary. It's safe, it's virtually foolproof, and so it's less fun to play this way.

ANIMAL HOUSES

Animal houses only become available after you've completed the relevant research. There are four types of animal houses: Insect House, Reptile House, Primate House (home to smaller species of monkeys), and Aviary (birds). Once you've got these four types, you can continue to research new types of animal house *exhibits*. For instance, the basic Reptile House contains an exhibit called Reptiles of the Rainforest. Further research will enable you to switch the exhibit inside your existing Reptile House to Deadly Snakes of the World—or, alternately, to build a second Reptile House for the newly available exhibit. Naturally, the more advanced exhibit types provide a bigger happiness boost for the visiting zoo guests. You can check on these by clicking the house in question and studying its information panel.

Each animal house counts as an extra attraction in your zoo. At the same time, building an animal house is much less expensive than constructing an animal exhibit (see Chapter 2). It comes complete with all the necessary bells and whistles and does not require maintenance by a zookeeper. Chapters 5 and 6 contain more details about animal houses and the exhibits inside.

CARING FOR ANIMALS

As a human being who has been around for a while, you probably know enough about caring for animals to dive right into the game and do a respectable job. However, all of us are subject to fits of ideological frenzy that cause us to neglect certain fundamentals. For instance, you might be so intent on making your male panda and female panda do a bit of business together (a winning condition in the final scenario!) that you forget about all your other animals. The best way to prevent disaster is to set things up so that you can indeed forget about all the other animals, and yet nothing bad will happen. Here's how to make things run smoothly in the care department even when you don't care.

☝ Place exhibit entrances thoughtfully. It's possible to greatly increase zookeeper efficiency by placing exhibit entrances close to each other. Chapter 2 discusses this in detail, and Chapter 4 contains info on zookeeper management. Note that even given the best gate placement you'll have to intervene now and then, like a real zoo manager, and tell the zookeeper what he should do next.

👋 Conduct appropriate research (see Figure 3.2). As explained in Chapter 5, research subjects are grouped into Research and Conservation. Practically everything under Research (animal shelters, staff education, animal care, and animal enrichment) contributes in one way or another to animal care, period. Some items in the Conservation research menu also affect animal happiness (exhibit foliage). See Chapter 5 for more details.

👋 Hire enough zookeepers. There's only one sure way of hiring enough zookeepers, and that's to hire slightly more than enough. Some animals require more care than others; in late scenarios and big freeform games, you'll find that you have to dedicate zookeepers to certain high-maintenance zoo stars. Having a single zookeeper care for just one exhibit is expensive, but you may have no other choice if the exhibit in question contains a large number of animals.

FIGURE 3.2:

All of these options are means to one end: happier animals.

The following sections examine each aspect of animal care in detail.

ANIMAL SENSITIVITY

Animals don't all adapt to captivity equally well. In *Zoo Tycoon*, this factor is accounted for in two ways:

🐾 Each species has a habitat suitability threshold that you must meet when building an exhibit; otherwise, the animal will become unhappy. Note that an animal's emotional changes take time; it won't become angry or deliriously happy overnight.

🐾 Every once in a while, the game runs a "captivity check" on all the animals in your zoo: Treat it as a flash of awareness on the part of the poor, dumb beast, during which it realizes it isn't free to go where it pleases. This results in a small but meaningful decrease in the animal's happiness. Fortunately, animals have short memories, and given a good habitat they quickly return to their former equilibrium. (Remember, however, that some animals need *numerous* companions to ensure their happiness.)

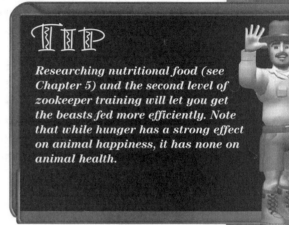

TIP

Researching nutritional food (see Chapter 5) and the second level of zookeeper training will let you get the beasts fed more efficiently. Note that while hunger has a strong effect on animal happiness, it has none on animal health.

Animal sensitivity may be a concern when you're on a tight budget and need a species that will happily rough it for a few months. The entries on the individual animals in "Stars of the Show," discussed later in this chapter, always include a relevant comment (see Appendix A for numerical values).

Animals are sensitive to the happiness of their companions within the exhibit. If one of several animals in an exhibit becomes unhappy, there's a chance other animals will become unhappy, too. This stresses the need for the prompt resolution of any animal unhappiness issues; if you don't act quickly, there might be a sudden epidemic of unhappiness!

ANIMAL HUNGER

They have to eat, don't they? You don't have to worry about the amount; the zookeeper automatically distributes however much is appropriate. What you do have to worry about is meal timing. Animals like being hungry even less than you do. Some animals get hungry more quickly than others; naturally, they require more maintenance. However, note that frequent meals do not *have* to mean equally frequent poo production, so to speak. You know—different strokes for different folks. You'll have to adjust the number of exhibits under each zookeeper's care accordingly. The individual animal entries outlined later on in this chapter include relevant observations.

When an animal is hungry and cannot find any food, you'll see the appropriate message in eye-catching red. Locate the hungry animal by clicking the message, and see what the problem is. Occasionally, it's caused by the poor beast being too dumb to find its food; pick it up and put it right on top of the meal, then adjust objects inside the exhibit so that all animals have easy access to the area where the zookeeper places food. If there's no food in the exhibit, pick up the nearest zookeeper and put him inside. He'll automatically place food right away, for he's a smart guy, and knows that this is the best way to ensure that he himself remains uneaten.

In order to ensure that animals can always find food easily, you should engage in a little detective work. Watch an exhibit for a while and you'll see where the animals tend to gather (often near fresh water) and where the zookeeper places food upon entering the exhibit. Moving the exhibit gate appropriately will make the zookeeper place food near the animals' gathering place.

ANIMAL HEALTH

Not all animals are equal in this respect; some are markedly more robust than others. As you might suspect, the fragile giant panda is the sickliest of the lot—20 times more so than an elephant! There are many variations in between; once again, the individual animal entries later on in this chapter contain appropriate comments.

When an animal is sick, you'll be alerted by a red message to that effect. You should immediately undertake emergency action; pausing the game is advised. Locate the sick animal by clicking the message; then pick up a zookeeper and transfer him to the animal's exhibit. As always, the zookeeper opens proceedings by placing food; then he'll proceed to heal the sick animal. If multiple animals are sick within the exhibit, you must make sure the zookeeper heals all of them by repeatedly picking him up and placing him back inside; zookeepers show a tendency to run from veterinarian duties.

ANIMAL STIMULATION

Animals may not read books or appreciate movies, but they do appreciate a bit of fun. All animals require some stimulation; more highly strung animals like the monkeys need quite a lot, and may indeed become unhappy without it, even if their other needs are met.

Animals can be stimulated in several ways:

- **Visits from the zookeeper.** Zookeepers with first-level training are better at making animals happy.

- **Presence of other animals.** As noted earlier, some animals require companionship more than others; however, even solitary animals such as the polar bear appreciate the presence of a mate. All monkeys are particularly demanding in this respect; a single primate will become unhappy even given the best exhibit possible, with a dedicated zookeeper dancing for its entertainment.

- **Animal toys.** Most of these are only available after you've conducted the appropriate research.

There's also such a thing as negative stimulation. How would you like to have 20 strangers watching your every move, hour after hour? Even the most vain animal star can be made uncomfortable by too many staring faces, and some animals are quite sensitive in this respect. You'll find appropriate comments in the entries on the individual animals in the next section. Note that not all animals that appear in the game can be adopted; they might be accompanying a special guest that enters your zoo without paying admission (see Figure 3.3).

FIGURE 3.3:

In games that last 12 months or longer, come Christmas you'll see Santa pass through your zoo in a sled pulled by reindeer.

Stars of the Show

The entries that follow describe, in turn, each of the animal species available in *Zoo Tycoon*. For ease of reference, they are arranged exactly as they are in the game.

Note that the appendices at the end of the guide also contain much useful animal data in table form. However, sometimes it takes longer to read a table than it does to read a paragraph, and it's certainly harder to link relevant facts together by looking at columns of numbers. Each of the following individual animal descriptions provides a portrait that should help you decide whether to acquire that species.

Animal Portraits

Each animal portrait follows the same format, starting with the animal's name. This is followed by:

- **Attractiveness:** This entry contains two numerical values separated by slashes. The first number refers to a single adult animal, and the second number to a single baby animal.

- **Minimum cost:** This represents the cost involved in buying the minimum number of animals that is required for happiness to reign inside the exhibit. Note that sometimes you can economize a little; for instance, zebras happily accept gazelles as companions, and gazelles cost less than zebras.

- **Animals in exhibit/shelter:** This states the smallest/biggest number of animals allowable in a happy exhibit and their favorite type of shelter. Remember that all animals are happy with concrete and wooden houses (the larger the house, the better), but will still prefer a special type of shelter if available. Some animals (for example, the saltwater crocodile) do not require a shelter.

- **Manageability:** This entry deals with the amount of trouble involved in maintaining an exhibit of the species. It includes such factors as animal hunger, sanitary habits, health, sensitivity, etc. The level of difficulty is multiplied by the average number of animals in an exhibit (you'll always want two—one of each sex—and can be required to have at least four).

🐾 **Exhibit:** This specifies exhibit type (for instance, there are two kinds of savannah, Australian and African) and defines the minimum amount of space required by a single animal of the discussed species. The percentage given at the end of this entry indicates the minimum exhibit suitability—i.e., the level below which the animal will become unhappy.

🐾 **Habitat:** This entry specifies the optimum terrain mix inside the animal's exhibit and tells you how much terrain should feature rocks and/or foliage (including the animal's favorite foliage).

🐾 **Comments:** These simply give extra information about the animal and tips on the timing of its acquisition.

Keep in mind that the game itself also contains plenty of interesting and helpful information about the individual species!

Savannah Animals

This is the largest group of animals in *Zoo Tycoon:* it includes no less than 18 animal species. All but two of these are from the African savannah; there are three carnivorous cats, two species of birds, and one extremely special species that is discussed in a separate section at the end of this chapter.

Herbivores from the African savannah are the right choice when you want to build an exhibit containing several different species. Although the exhibit concerned is invariably big and expensive both to build and to maintain (it usually requires a dedicated zookeeper), it's still worth the effort. Remember that exhibiting four or more species in the same exhibit gives guests an extra happiness boost (see Chapter 6 for more details).

African Elephant

Attractiveness: 50/150

Minimum cost: $5,000

Animals in exhibit/shelter: 2–6, elephant shelter

Manageability: Slightly difficult

Exhibit: African savannah, 50 tiles per animal, 65% suitability

---

Habitat: 65% savannah grass, 10% dirt, 10% sand, 15% fresh water; 2% rocks, 5% trees—baobab, yellow fever acacia, thorn bush

Comments: The true king of animals requires a lot of space and pampering to keep it happy; it's definitely an expensive choice. Its appetite and sanitary habits will make the assigned zookeeper pretty busy, which is all to the good: Elephants don't like captivity and frequent happiness-boosting visits from the keeper help keep them contented. Elephants mix well with some animals from the African savannah; however, their personal space requirements make their inclusion in large mixed exhibits impractical. They don't reproduce easily.

All the expense and trouble involved in maintaining an elephant exhibit is fully repaid in increased guest attraction. Besides, no big zoo is really complete without an elephant, and these animals are exceptionally healthy and long-lived; you'll want to adopt a couple whenever it's affordable.

OLIVE BABOON

Attractiveness: 10/30

Minimum cost: $2,700

Animals in exhibit/shelter: 3–20, concrete or wooden house

Manageability: Somewhat difficult

Exhibit: African savannah, 15 tiles per animal, 70% suitability

Habitat: 90% savannah grass, 10% dirt; 4% rocks, 15% foliage—baobab, thorn bush

Comments: Although all primates like each other, don't try combining a baboon with a chimp or a mandrill—the latter two prefer a rainforest habitat. This animal is the cheapest of the primate species featured in *Zoo Tycoon*; its exhibit (like all exhibits featuring primates) is bound to draw plenty of zoo guests. The olive baboon's eating and digestive habits are pretty easygoing; however, it is a rather sickly animal, and slightly moody. It's somewhat sensitive to crowds, but reproduces fairly easily; if you build the ideal exhibit, you may get away with adopting just two baboons of different sexes, and they'll quickly produce the third animal needed to keep them happy.

Overall, the olive baboon is one of the easier primates to manage and is often the logical choice for your first outdoor primate exhibit.

PLAINS ZEBRA

Attractiveness: 5/15

Minimum cost: $2,400

Animals in exhibit/shelter: 3–20, lean-to

Manageability: Very easy

Exhibit: African savannah, 15 tiles per animal, 50% suitability

Habitat: 95% savannah grass, 5% fresh water—long savannah grass, umbrella acacia

Comments: This is one of the most easygoing animals in *Zoo Tycoon*. It is happy in a relatively poor exhibit, undemanding in its feeding and digestive habits, and it also has one of the game's most entertaining "happy" animations, bounding over the grass in joyful leaps. It is perfect as part of a big, mixed African savannah exhibit; in fact, the only downside to adopting a zebra is its low individual attractiveness. However, this is offset by the fact that it reproduces quickly as long as habitat conditions are slightly better than the required minimum.

You'll almost always have a few zebras in your zoo; some scenario games highlight this animal, and it's always a good buy in freeform games.

BLACK RHINOCEROS

Attractiveness: 10/30

Minimum cost: $1,200

Animals in exhibit/shelter: 1–2, stable

Manageability: Easy

Exhibit: African savannah, 50 tiles per animal, 70% suitability

Habitat: 85% savannah grass, 10% dirt, 5% fresh water; 2% rocks, 9% foliage—umbrella acacia tree, thorn bush

Comments: An exhibit devoted solely to the rhino is bound to be one of the least attractive in your zoo. However, as explained in Chapter 2, such plain exhibits have their uses, too. Otherwise, you may include a solitary rhino in a mixed savannah exhibit; its foliage preferences can be a little hard to reconcile with the other animals', but like its savannah friends the black rhino is just tolerant enough to make a happy habitat compromise possible. It does need a lot of space to itself plus a strong exhibit barrier, and its dietary habits require a significant amount of attention. On the plus side, it's very long-lived.

Some scenarios highlight the rhino, so you'll see for yourself what it feels like to own one. It's not a hot choice in freeform games.

THOMSON'S GAZELLE

Attractiveness: 5/15

Minimum cost: $1,500

Animals in exhibit/shelter: 3–25, lean-to

Manageability: Very easy

Exhibit: African savannah, 15 tiles per animal, 50% suitability

Habitat: 95% savannah grass, 5% fresh water; 1% rocks, 2% foliage—long savannah grass

Comments: This is probably one of the most endearing animals in the game. It's very inexpensive, very easygoing, very quick to reproduce—it's very everything except for durable; its life span is quite short. However, you can always count on having plenty of young gazelles if the habitat meets their tolerant requirements. The animation showing a happy Thomson's gazelle is particularly jolly.

This animal is a very good choice in almost every game of *Zoo Tycoon*; usually it makes sense to mix it with its friends from the African savannah. Its low attractiveness is a little deceiving, since there will almost always be a couple of baby gazelles around—provided you did a good job with the habitat.

COMMON WILDEBEEST

Attractiveness: 5/15

Minimum cost: $3,000

Animals in exhibit/shelter: 3–25, lean-to

Manageability: Easy

Exhibit: African savannah, 15 tiles per animal, 60% suitability

Habitat: 80% savannah grass, 10% dirt, 5% sand, 5% water; 1% rocks, 2% foliage—long savannah grass, white thorn acacia

Comments: Like other hoofed quadrupeds from the African savannah, the wildebeest is of an uncomplaining and tolerant nature. It's very slightly more demanding than a zebra or a gazelle—being a bigger beast it eats more, and so on. It reproduces easily; given its average life span, you'll quickly end up with herds of 5–6 wildebeest even if you initially purchase just one animal of each sex.

This is yet another good choice for a mixed savannah exhibit.

GIRAFFE

Attractiveness: 25/75

Minimum cost: $3,200

Animals in exhibit/shelter: 2–10, giraffe shelter

Manageability: Average

Exhibit: African savannah, 35 tiles per animal, 70% suitability

Habitat: 83% savannah grass, 10% dirt, 5% sand, 2% fresh water; 1% rocks, 13% foliage—umbrella acacia tree, baobab

Comments: This graceful animal enjoys more fame than most of its savannah friends, a fact that's reflected in its attractiveness rating. It is a relatively expensive species to acquire. It has a healthy appetite and a quick-functioning digestive system; animal for animal, it's more difficult to care for than the African buffalo or the wildebeest. Its love of foliage makes it impractical to include a giraffe in a big mixed savannah exhibit; remember that ideally you want all of your animals happy enough to reproduce. Giraffes are a little difficult in this respect; they dislike captivity. A zookeeper's frequent visits can help if everything else fails!

Luckily, an exhibit devoted to giraffes has enough pull to be a meaningful attraction, especially once a baby giraffe shows up on the scene. One of the early scenarios highlights this animal, and you'll want to adopt a couple in most freeform games.

AFRICAN BUFFALO

Attractiveness: 5/15

Minimum cost: $2,400

Animals in exhibit/shelter: 2–10, stable

Manageability: Average

Exhibit type and size: African savannah, 20 tiles per animal

Habitat: 80% savannah grass, 10% dirt, 5% sand, 5% fresh water; 5% foliage—long savannah grass. No rocks!

Comments: This is the largest model in the African savannah hoofed quadruped line. It's correspondingly slightly more difficult to care for, unfortunately without a matching increase in attractiveness. Apart from that, it shares the characteristics of its African friends; for example, it's tolerant of its habitat, which makes it a good candidate for mixed savannah exhibits. However, it needs slightly more space than the smaller hoofed animals and doesn't reproduce quite as easily.

    The low attractiveness of an exhibit devoted solely to those animals means you'll almost always adopt them for mixed exhibits; you may need to upgrade the exhibit barriers. African buffaloes do not play a special role in any of the scenario games.

HIPPOPOTAMUS

Attractiveness: 50/150

Minimum cost: $2,400

Animals in exhibit/shelter: 2–10, none

Manageability: Somewhat difficult

Exhibit: African savannah, 35 tiles per animal, 70% suitability

Habitat: 70% fresh water, 15% savannah grass, 15% dirt; 1% rocks, 1% foliage—water reed, thorn bush, acacia tree

Comments: This animal is one of *Zoo Tycoon*'s minor stars. Although its habitat requirements make it totally unsuitable for large mixed savannah exhibits, you'll find that flamingos and hippos suit each other perfectly. A flamingo/hippo exhibit will generate considerable interest; place it accordingly. You may find it necessary to assign a dedicated zookeeper, as hippos are voracious eaters and have very efficient digestion! This tends to be the only drawback to a hippo exhibit, as they are tolerant of crowds and of captivity, and enjoy good health. Their life span is only average, which is a bit disappointing, especially since this animal is slow to reproduce.

You'll definitely want a hippo exhibit in all of your zoos except for selected scenario games. It is a crowd-pleaser, and adding flamingos will offset some of the cost of the extra-strong exhibit barriers you'll need.

Lion

Attractiveness: 30/60

Minimum cost: $2,100

Animals in exhibit/shelter: 3–10, rock cave

Manageability: Easy

Exhibit: African savannah, 20 tiles per animal, 70% suitability

Habitat: 83% savannah grass, 10% dirt, 5% sand, 2% fresh water; 1% rocks, 13% foliage—umbrella acacia tree, baobab

Comments: This animal, democratically voted the king of animals, is one of the best choices you can make in any scenario or freeform game. A lion exhibit will always be very attractive to guests, since investing in a male and two females quickly results in numerous baby lions. This particular king needs little pampering; it's tolerant of crowds, clean, and easygoing. On the whole, it appears to mind captivity very little.

A lion exhibit is a particularly good choice when starting a new freeform game; this species is also highlighted in several scenarios. You'll probably want to adopt a few lions even if it's not a scenario goal.

Cheetah

Attractiveness: 20/60

Minimum cost: $1,600

Animals in exhibit/shelter: 1–3, rock cave

Manageability: Somewhat difficult

Exhibit: African savannah, 50 tiles per animal, 70% suitability

Habitat: 90% savannah grass, 10% dirt; 2% rocks, 2% foliage—thorn bush

Comments: This cat, being the fastest animal in the world, requires as much space as an elephant. Caring for it can be troublesome, too; although clean, the cheetah dislikes captivity and has a moody disposition. It's somewhat sensitive to crowds and quite sickly. Getting it to reproduce may prove difficult.

The cheetah stars in a couple of scenarios. In a freeform game, it's not a very hot choice; the big exhibit gives a poor return in terms of generated attractiveness per terrain tile and yet has to figure prominently in your planning.

LEOPARD

Attractiveness: 40/120

Minimum cost: $1,100

Animals in exhibit/shelter: 1–2, rock cave

Manageability: Average

Exhibit: African savannah, 35 tiles per animal, 90% suitability

Habitat: 70% savannah grass, 20% rainforest, 5% dirt, 5% fresh water; 6% rocks, 15% foliage—baobab, white thorn acacia tree

Comments: While the leopard can't equal the lion as an exhibit choice, it's definitely a better bet than the cheetah. It's a little bit sensitive in all respects. Setting up a good exhibit costs quite a bit of coin, too; fortunately all these disadvantages are at least partly offset by this animal's high individual attractiveness. Note that the average lion exhibit will still command more attention than two leopards!

Given a well-designed exhibit, the leopard is not hard to care for. It enjoys average health and an average life span; you'll have to adopt new animals to keep the exhibit going. This species is prominently featured in several scenarios, and you'll generally want to own a leopard exhibit when playing freeform games.

SPOTTED HYENA

Attractiveness: 15/45

Minimum cost: $3,600

Animals in exhibit/shelter: 3–15, rock cave

Manageability: Average

Exhibit: African savannah, 20 tiles per animal, 80% suitability

Habitat: 75% savannah grass, 10% dirt, 10% sand, 5% fresh water; 1% rocks, 2% foliage—umbrella acacia tree, acacia tree

Comments: In animal folklore this species is widely reviled for its "cowardly" character (see the in-game Animal Facts panel). However, it's still a reasonably attractive addition to your zoo. It's average in most respects such as adaptation to captivity, reproduction, health, and life span; however, it should be remembered that despite its relatively small size the hyena has the appetite and animal poo–producing capacity of a lion.

The hyena does not play a significant role in any of the game scenarios. In spite of its unappealing character, though, it's still a sound addition to any zoo. The efficient tycoon does not let animal morals interfere with business; put its exhibit next to a washroom if you must express your disapproval (it won't mind).

GREATER FLAMINGO

Attractiveness: 10/30

Minimum cost: $1,500

Animals in exhibit/shelter: 2–20, none

Manageability: Easy

Exhibit: African savannah, 15 tiles per animal, 70% suitability

Habitat: 60% fresh water, 20% dirt, 10% savannah grass, 10% sand; 0% rocks, 0% foliage

Comments: This graceful bird is best acquired as part of a hippo/flamingo exhibit. However, an exhibit containing just flamingos commands reasonable attention in itself. In spite of being just a bird, it wisely knows what side its bread is buttered on and won't take off into the wild blue yonder; no special adjustments to the exhibit are necessary. It is fairly easy to care for, being tolerant of captivity and crowds, and it enjoys relatively good health. It enjoys an average life span and reproduces relatively easily. Interestingly, it has an appetite and food-processing capabilities that equal the lion's.

Greater flamingos do not play an important role in any of the scenarios. At the same time, their good dollars-to-attractiveness ratio makes them a safe choice in any game. As previously mentioned, they are best acquired to further boost the attractiveness of a hippo exhibit.

OSTRICH

Attractiveness: 5/15

Minimum cost: $2,200

Animals in exhibit/shelter: 2–12, lean-to

Manageability: Easy

Exhibit: African savannah, 20 tiles per animal, 60% suitability

Habitat: 90% savannah grass, 5% dirt, 5% fresh water; 2% rocks, 3% foliage—long savannah grass, thorn bush

Comments: *Zoo Tycoon*'s ostriches are brave birds that do not have the legendary tendency to stick their heads in the sand in dangerous situations; in fact, they dislike this terrain type. They do not command a great deal of attention from zoo guests and are best acquired for big mixed African savannah exhibits. Ostriches are amiable birds that are easygoing in all areas: They aren't particularly sensitive to crowds or captivity, enjoy good health, and reproduce fairly easily. Their life span, while below average, is still better than the greater flamingo's.

The ostrich does not play a headline role in any of the game's set scenarios. Since their attractiveness is low, it doesn't make sense to build an exhibit solely around them. Note that ostriches cannot fly.

AFRICAN WARTHOG

Attractiveness: 10/30

Minimum cost: $1,200

Animals in exhibit/shelter: 2–6, burrow

Manageability: Easy

Exhibit: African savannah, 20 tiles per animal, 70% suitability

Habitat: 70% dirt, 20% savannah grass, 5% sand, 5% fresh water; 6% rocks, 2% foliage—thorn bush, long savannah grass

Comments: This little piggy likes dirt! Unfortunately, the love of dirt makes the warthog unsuitable for inclusion in big, reproduction-happy mixed African savannah exhibits. In spite of its terrain preferences, the warthog is a clean animal with a restrained appetite; it's healthy, adapts well to captivity, and has an average inclination to reproduce during its average life span. However, it's very sensitive to crowds and should be placed in exhibits that allow it to hide from sight.

Adopting warthogs has one big advantage: Building an exhibit for these animals is fairly cheap. However, they'll never be one of your zoo's big attractions. They do not play a significant role in any of the set scenarios.

RED KANGAROO

Attractiveness: 25/105

Minimum cost: $600

Animals in exhibit/shelter: 1–3, lean-to

Manageability: Very easy

Exhibit: Australian savannah, 20 tiles per animal, 60% suitability

Habitat: 60% savannah grass, 30% dirt, 8% sand, 2% fresh water; 2% rocks, 4% foliage—hard quandong tree, eucalyptus tree, grass tree, red gum tree

Comments: This species from the land down under is a real crowd-pleaser, and although it is not highlighted by any of the scenario games, it's invariably a good choice. It's cheap to acquire and its exhibit is quite inexpensive; furthermore, it is fairly easy to care for. It has an average appetite and poo-producing capability, enjoys good health during its average life span, and once truly happy breeds easily. However, the red kangaroo's happiness is meaningfully affected by the audience it tends to draw; plan the exhibit accordingly.

You'll want to adopt this species whenever it's available; in freeform games, that means a wait, but your patience will be amply rewarded.

GRASSLAND ANIMALS

Exhibits built for grassland animals can utilize the existing terrain of many zoo maps in the game, but unfortunately this group includes just one species: the American Bison.

AMERICAN BISON

Attractiveness: 10/30

Minimum cost: $4,500

Animals in exhibit/shelter: 3–10, stable

Manageability: Average

Exhibit: North American grassland, 20 tiles per animal, 70% suitability

Habitat: 95% grass, 5% fresh water; 3% rocks, 3% foliage—broadleaf bush.

Comments: The sole representative of grassland species is easy to care for, despite its size (which necessitates sturdy exhibit barriers). Although the costs of creating a good habitat are fairly low, a bison exhibit is hardly a bargain; it needs to be quite large to maximize its attractiveness, and the adoption itself isn't cheap. The American bison adapts well to captivity, reproduces easily, and doesn't mind crowds. On the minus side, its health is unexceptional, and it comes with a big appetite and a big appetite's usual consequences (though they are less dire than with some animals of comparable size). Its life span is just average, which is a little disappointing.

The bison is highlighted in one of the earlier scenarios. It's not the best choice in freeform games because of its exhibit's relatively low attractiveness.

DECIDUOUS FOREST ANIMALS

There are two representatives of this group in the game: the black bear and the moose. The term "deciduous forest animals" is a little misleading, because both species require a certain amount of coniferous forest terrain in their habitats. Note that Mystery Beast #1 (described at the end of this chapter) is rumored to inhabit deciduous forests, too.

BLACK BEAR

Attractiveness: 20/60

Minimum cost: $850

Animals in exhibit/shelter: 1–3, rock cave

Manageability: Average

Exhibit: Deciduous forest, 35 tiles per animal, 70% suitability

Habitat: 60% deciduous forest, 30% coniferous forest; 7% rocks, 20% foliage—trembling aspen, white oak, birch, maple

Comments: This species is a good example of how misleading an animal's adoption price may be—its exhibit is a costly one. It requires plenty of foliage and strong barriers. The black bear doesn't like big crowds or captivity, and its health, life span, and ease of reproduction are just average. While an individual animal of this species commands respectable attention from zoo guests, its exhibit as such isn't a big attraction.

One of the earlier scenarios highlights this animal, and in spite of its low exhibit attractiveness you'll still want to have it in most of your zoos. There are only two standard deciduous forest choices!

MOOSE

Attractiveness: 25/75

Minimum cost: $700

Animals in exhibit/shelter: 1–3, stable

Manageability: Easy

Exhibit: Deciduous forest, 20 tiles per animal, 75% suitability

Habitat: 50% deciduous forest, 20% coniferous forest, 20% grass, 10% fresh water; 2% rocks, 14% foliage—weeping willow, white oak

Comments: This is the more attractive of the two standard deciduous forest species, and its exhibit is significantly cheaper to build than one that would keep a black bear happy. The moose is a docile animal that adapts very well to captivity, doesn't mind crowds, and enjoys an average health and life span. It reproduces fairly easily when in a good habitat.

The moose makes an appearance in the first game scenario. It's a good economical choice in any game, and you'll also enjoy the fact that moose of different sex look different.

Coniferous Forest Animals

This group includes three species, two of which (the grizzly and the Siberian tiger) like mountainous terrain. If the zoo map you're playing has hilly areas, plan your zoo accordingly! Significant changes to terrain elevation can add quite a few dollars to the cost of setting up an exhibit.

Siberian Tiger

Attractiveness: 30/90

Minimum cost: $2,000

Animals in exhibit/shelter: 2–3, rock cave

Manageability: Easy

Exhibit: Coniferous forest, 35 tiles per animal, 70% suitability

Habitat: 40% coniferous forest, 40% snow, 15% gray rock, 5% fresh water; 2% rocks, 12% foliage—Chinese fir tree, pine shrub

Comments: This animal is just attractive enough to justify the considerable cost involved in setting up the exhibit. Its terrain preferences include fairly steep slopes that almost always require adjustments to the existing map. However, the effort pays off nicely: Once the habitat is to its liking, the Siberian tiger breeds easily, producing two cubs at a time. It adapts extremely well to captivity and has a normal appetite for an animal of its size; it's also quite clean and not especially bothered by crowds. Siberian tigers live to a very old age if their less-than-perfect health is given proper attention, and you'll make a few dollars on the side from the sale of these animals—certainly enough to cover the extra exhibit cost.

The Siberian tiger plays a star role in several of the game's scenarios. It's also often a good choice in other games. Its exhibit is a little troublesome to set up, but more than pays for itself in the long run.

GRIZZLY BEAR

Attractiveness: 35/105

Minimum cost: $1,000

Animals in exhibit/shelter: 1–3, rock cave

Manageability: Average

Exhibit: Coniferous forest, 50 tiles per animal, 70% suitability

Habitat: 50% coniferous forest, 20% deciduous forest, 10% brown rock, 10% fresh water; 7% rocks, 20% foliage—yellow cedar, western red cedar, white spruce

Comments: The grizzly is a more demanding animal than the black bear, but returns bigger dividends. It likes steep slopes and plenty of space; given the necessity for strong barriers, a grizzly exhibit is fairly expensive. It is a slightly moody animal with a dislike for large crowds, and it's endowed with a good appetite and correspondingly efficient digestion. Getting it to reproduce may be somewhat difficult; success is rewarded with two cubs.

The grizzly plays an important role in a couple of the game scenarios. Its shyness may cause problems if you don't build the exhibit accordingly (i.e., with solid barriers hiding the grizzly from too many eyes). Adopting a grizzly is best postponed until you're quite comfortable financially.

GRAY WOLF

Attractiveness: 10/30

Minimum cost: $3,600

Animals in exhibit/shelter: 4–20, rock cave

Manageability: Somewhat difficult

Exhibit: Coniferous forest, 35 tiles per animal, 80% suitability

Habitat: 50% coniferous forest, 25% grass, 20% deciduous forest, 5% fresh water; 1% rocks, 12% foliage—white spruce tree, lodge pine tree, yellow cedar

Comments: This animal requires an expensive exhibit: it has to be big, and much of that area needs to be covered with foliage. Gray wolves have very good appetites, so feeding a pack of these animals (and cleaning up after them) keeps zookeepers busy. Once the rather exacting habitat requirements of this animal are met (it's not too fond of crowds and captivity, either), it breeds easily. Gray wolves enjoy very good health and live to a ripe old age.

Gray wolves aren't highlighted by any of the scenarios, but their exhibit can be one of the bigger zoo attractions. Its size will require special consideration when you're planning your zoo.

TROPICAL RAINFOREST ANIMALS

This is the second-largest group of animals in the game. It consists of no less than 11 species, 6 of which have to be researched before they become available (Conservation, Endangered Animals). Tropical rainforest animals play a very prominent role in several scenarios; you'll have to know how to make them *really* happy in order to win! Note that the rainforest species presented in *Zoo Tycoon* come from three different continents; they're presented here in the order in which they appear in the game once all research has been completed.

MANDRILL

Attractiveness: 12/36

Minimum cost: $3,900

Animals in exhibit/shelter: 3–20, concrete or wooden house

Manageability: Somewhat difficult

Exhibit type and size: African rainforest, 15 tiles per animal, 80% suitability

Habitat: 85% rainforest, 10% grass, 5% dirt; 4% rocks, 15% foliage—elephant ear tree

Comments: An exhibit containing many happy mandrills can be one of the main attractions in your zoo! Of course, caring for an exhibit that contains many animals is more difficult, especially since the mandrill, being a primate, is a little tricky to handle. Its restrained appetite and cleanliness help a little; however, it is somewhat sensitive to captivity and to crowds, and has delicate health that needs regular attention. Proper mandrill care is rewarded with a very long life span and swift reproduction; it's not necessary to buy more than a male and two females to maximize the attraction of this exhibit.

This species is not singled out by any of the scenarios, but building a primate exhibit is always a good proposition, and you'll want as many of these as is feasible in any game.

CHIMPANZEE

Attractiveness: 15/45

Minimum cost: $4,500

Animals in exhibit/shelter: 3–15, concrete or wooden house

Manageability: Average

Exhibit type and size: African rainforest, 15 tiles per animal, 70% suitability

Habitat: 85% rainforest, 10% grass, 5% dirt; 4% rocks, 20% foliage—orchid tree

Comments: An exhibit containing chimpanzees is always one of the bigger attractions in your zoo. Chimps are slightly easier to care for than mandrills; while they dislike captivity to a similar degree, they aren't as mindful of crowds and enjoy slightly better health (it's still fragile, though). These primates have a relatively small appetite and are generally clean; of course, a large number will be proportionally more difficult to care for. Once their habitat requirements are met, chimpanzees reproduce easily, and given good health care survive to a very old age.

This species is highlighted in one of the earlier scenarios and is a good choice in any game. Remember that it is highly attractive to zoo guests; place and build the exhibit accordingly. Warning: Do not mix chimpanzees and mandrills, even though the two species have highly compatible habitat preferences—they don't like each other.

LOWLAND GORILLA

Attractiveness: 25/75

Minimum cost: $5,000

Animals in exhibit/shelter: 2–10, concrete or wooden house

Manageability: Difficult

Exhibit type and size: African rainforest, 20 tiles per animal, 85% suitability

Habitat: 70% rainforest, 20% grass, 10% dirt; 6% rocks, 15% foliage—elephant ear tree

Comments: The lowland gorilla is often the first species to be researched under Endangered Animals. While an exhibit containing these apes can be a huge hit with zoo guests, caring for it is far from easy. The gorilla's habitat has to suit its tastes exactly; on top of that it has poor health, doesn't like captivity or big crowds, and has a big appetite coupled with a hardworking digestive system. Getting it to reproduce is difficult; fortunately these animals, given good health care, can survive to a very old age. Do not try putting gorillas together with chimps in the same exhibit; although the two species are compatible, the gorillas' sensitivity makes it a bad idea.

You can avoid having to care for gorillas in the set scenarios; however, the gorilla exhibit's high attractiveness makes having one a big boon for your zoo. The wise thing to do is to postpone adopting gorillas until you're flush with cash and can afford expensive exhibit fine-tuning.

OKAPI

Attractiveness: 50/150

Minimum cost: $1,800

Animals in exhibit/shelter: 1–2, lean-to

Manageability: Difficult

Exhibit type and size: African rainforest, 20 tiles per animal, 80% suitability

Habitat: 85% rainforest, 8% grass, 5% dirt; 1% rocks, 20% foliage—orchid tree, rainforest bush

Comments: This is the penultimate endangered species to be researched. Its pull with zoo guests is disproportionately weak in relation to the amount of care it entails. Building a highly suitable habitat with the game paused is a must; these animals are initially very unhappy to find themselves in a zoo, and given their poor health may quickly succumb to sickness. The okapi has a reasonably good appetite and good digestion; however, it intensely dislikes both crowds and captivity, and getting it to reproduce is quite a task.

Making okapi reproduce is a winning condition of one of the game's scenarios. From a business standpoint, an okapi exhibit doesn't make much sense, but the exotic looks of this animal will probably tempt you to risk adoption. If so, make sure you've got enough money to afford an extra zookeeper—it's a good idea to dedicate one exclusively to the okapi exhibit.

WHITE BENGAL TIGER

Attractiveness: 70/210

Minimum cost: $3,000

Animals in exhibit/shelter: 2–3, rock cave

Manageability: Average

Exhibit type and size: Southeast Asian rainforest, 35 tiles per animal, 70% suitability

Habitat: 70% rainforest, 15% grass, 10% fresh water, 5% dirt; 4% rocks, 20% foliage—mangrove tree, rainforest fern

Comments: The white Bengal tiger is the second endangered species you'll research. In this case, rarity does not imply difficult care, and the white Bengal tiger displays most of the amiable qualities of the big cats. It takes very well to captivity and doesn't mind crowds, but is of only average health and has a short life span. Luckily, once its habitat requirements are met it reproduces fairly easily. It has the appetite of the average big cat, but subdued poo-producing talents.

Making these cats reproduce is a goal of one of the scenarios. Otherwise, the white Bengal tiger is a good choice once it has been researched: It has great pull with the paying public! Take this into consideration when planning and placing the exhibit.

BENGAL TIGER

Attractiveness: 50/150

Minimum cost: $800

Animals in exhibit/shelter: 1–2, rock cave

Manageability: Easy

Exhibit type and size: Southeast Asian rainforest, 35 tiles per animal, 70% suitability

Habitat: 70% rainforest, 15% grass, 10% water, 5% dirt; 2% rocks, 20% foliage— mangrove tree, rainforest fern

Comments: This famous animal has been popularly voted yet another animal king; this time it's king of the jungle. In many ways, the Bengal tiger is similar to that other cat king, the lion: It adapts to captivity very easily, doesn't mind crowds, and enjoys good health. As expected, it has a healthy appetite and efficient digestion, but the low number of tigers per exhibit makes it easy to keep the exhibit clean. Once its habitat requirements are met, the Bengal tiger reproduces easily.

The Bengal tiger plays a starring role in a couple of scenarios and is a good choice in any game. The large amount of foliage and water in its habitat means that you must position the exhibit gate thoughtfully for easy zookeeper access.

BLACK LEOPARD

Attractiveness: 50/150

Minimum cost: $1,600

Animals in exhibit/shelter: 1–2, rock cave

Manageability: Somewhat difficult

Exhibit type and size: Southeast Asian rainforest, 20 tiles per animal, 90% suitability

Habitat: 85% rainforest, 10% grass, 5% dirt; 6% rocks, 15% foliage—foxtail palm, mangrove tree

Comments: This rare cat is the third species to be researched under Endangered Animals. It distinguishes itself by having a very moderate appetite with corresponding poo-making ability; its health and attitude to captivity are unexceptional, but don't present great problems, and it enjoys an average life span. However, like other leopards, this animal simply hates crowds, and this is one of the factors that make breeding these cats difficult.

As it happens, making black leopards reproduce is a winning condition of one of the game's scenarios. In freeform games, this species is a solid choice despite its shyness; just plan and place the exhibit appropriately.

CLOUDED LEOPARD

Attractiveness: 40/120

Minimum cost: $1,800

Animals in exhibit/shelter: 1–2, rock cave

Manageability: Somewhat difficult

Exhibit type and size: Southeast Asian rainforest, 35 tiles per animal, 90% suitability

Habitat: 80% rainforest, 20% grass, 5% dirt; 6% rocks, 15% foliage—mangrove tree, rainforest fern

Comments: This cat is shy! In addition to displaying a profound dislike for crowds, the clouded leopard is very finicky about its habitat and not overly fond of being captive. Making it reproduce can be a problem and may necessitate frequent morale-boosting visits from a zookeeper. Apart from that, this animal has a restrained appetite, is fairly clean, and enjoys an average life span.

Because its shyness limits the numbers of spectators, the clouded leopard isn't a very hot choice as an exhibit. In terms of attractiveness, it offers significantly less bang for your buck than the Bengal tiger. While it's highlighted in a couple of scenarios, in freeform games you shouldn't consider it until your zoo is comfortable financially—adding a clouded leopard exhibit often means having to hire an extra zookeeper.

JAGUAR

Attractiveness: 25/75

Minimum cost: $1,100

Animals in exhibit/shelter: 1–2, rock cave

Manageability: Somewhat difficult

Exhibit type and size: Southeast Asian rainforest, 20 tiles per animal, 90% suitability

Habitat: 75% rainforest, 13% dirt, 12% fresh water; 6% rocks, 20% foliage—kapok tree, ulmo tree

Comments: This South American carnivore is relatively troublesome and does not reward all the effort needed to make it happy with high attractiveness. It has a small appetite, is very clean, and adapts to captivity relatively well; at the same time it is sickly, hates crowds, has a short life span, and does not reproduce easily.

The jaguar is highlighted in one of the game's scenarios; when playing a freeform game, you should consider it only if you start running short of rainforest choices.

GIANT ANTEATER

Attractiveness: 10/30

Minimum Cost: $600

Animals in exhibit/shelter: 1–3, burrow

Manageability: Easy

Exhibit type and size: South American rainforest, 15 tiles per animal, 70% suitability

Habitat: 80% rainforest, 10% dirt, 8% grass, 2% fresh water; 0% rocks, 12% foliage—ulmo tree, llala palm

Comments: The anteater is one of the most economical choices you can make; a solitary specimen can survive happily in a small exhibit featuring a couple of trees and a shelter. However, building a 100% suitable habitat involves at least 50 tiles because of the fresh water requirement. Fortunately, anteaters aren't very fussy about their habitat; they also don't eat much and consequently are very clean. They have average sensitivity to crowds, and given the low adoption price would be ideal in almost every respect if not for their low attractiveness and short life span.

Acquiring an anteater is a wise move in scenarios whose winning conditions include a certain number of exhibits/animal species in your zoo.

HIGHLAND ANIMALS

Animals belonging to this group entail a bit of extra trouble because of the sharp slopes they need to have in their exhibits, which pretty much always necessitate expensive terrain adjustments. The five species listed below include two that have to be researched before they can be adopted. The descriptions follow the order in which animals appear on the adoption menu once all research has been completed.

Rumor has it that an extra mystery highland species will be released via the Web.

MARKHOR

Attractiveness: 10/30

Minimum cost: $2,800

Animals in exhibit/shelter: 2–7, lean-to

Manageability: Average

Exhibit type and size: Central Asian highlands, 20 tiles per animal, 90% suitability

Habitat: 60% gray rock, 30% snow, 5% grass, 5% fresh water; 8% rocks, 2% foliage—Himalayan birch, Himalayan pine

Comments: This exotic mountain goat tends to be a troublesome acquisition, partly because of its rather exacting habitat requirements. In addition to requiring steep mountain slopes within its exhibit, it has fairly delicate health, dislikes captivity, and isn't fond of crowds. It is a moderate eater and so on, does not reproduce very easily, and enjoys only an average life span. The expense-to-attractiveness ratio isn't encouraging.

The markhor does not play a special role in any of the game scenarios, and isn't a very happy choice in freeform games. Its acquisition is best left until new adoption choices shrink to just a few species.

Snow Leopard

Attractiveness: 55/165

Minimum cost: $2,400

Animals in exhibit/shelter: 1–2, snowy rock cave

Manageability: Difficult

Exhibit type and size: Central Asian highlands, 35 tiles per animal, 90% suitability

Habitat: 60% snow, 30% gray rock, 10% brown rock; 10% rocks, 1% foliage—Himalayan pine tree

Comments: The snow leopard is the fourth endangered species you'll research. It is a cranky cat that dislikes captivity and absolutely hates crowds; even a scattering of onlookers can send this animal into a funk. Its exhibit is expensive to build and calls for careful planning and placement. Apart from that, this is a very clean cat with an understated appetite and shaky health; if well cared for it has an average life span. It reproduces slowly and reluctantly.

Snow leopards are highlighted by one of the game's set scenarios. Otherwise, this is a fairly troublesome and risky choice without commensurate rewards.

Giant Panda

Attractiveness: 90/270

Minimum cost: $5,000

Animals in exhibit/shelter: 1–2, panda cave

Manageability: Very difficult

Exhibit type and size: Central Asian highlands, 20 tiles per animal, 70% suitability

Habitat: 80% coniferous, 8% grass, 5% gray rock, 5% snow, 2% water; 2% rocks, 13% foliage—bamboo, Himalayan birch, Himalayan pine tree

Comments: The giant panda is the last species in the Endangered Animal research queue. It is a very troublesome choice, and you shouldn't consider adopting one until you've also researched bamboo (Exhibit Foliage, Conservation). It has a ravenous appetite and amazing poo-producing ability. Very poor health and a hatred of both crowds and captivity mean that this animal rarely achieves the level of happiness needed for reproduction, which is both extremely difficult and slow to yield results. You must make sure that this animal's habitat is as perfect as you can make it the moment you complete the adoption; the great panda is extremely unhappy to start with.

As you've probably guessed by now, breeding giant pandas is the objective of the game's last scenario; the thorny road leading to success therein is described in Chapter 8. When playing a freeform game, make sure you've got reserves of cash, time, and patience before you adopt this animal. A dedicated zookeeper is a must!

IBEX

Attractiveness: 25/75

Minimum cost: $1,875

Animals in exhibit/shelter: 3–10, lean-to

Manageability: Average

Exhibit type and size: Central Asian highlands, 20 tiles per animal, 75% suitability

Habitat: 70% gray rock, 20% brown rock, 5% grass, 5% fresh water; 7% rocks, 1% foliage—Himalayan pine tree, Himalayan birch

Comments: This species is the safest, best bet among highland animal exhibits. Although setting up the exhibit is fairly expensive on account of both terrain-level adjustments and exhibit size, the return you get justifies the investment. An ibex exhibit with maxed-out attractiveness ranks among the top sights in your zoo! In addition, this species compares favorably to the markhor in almost every other area: It adapts well to captivity, enjoys robust health, and reproduces reasonably easily. It has a moderate appetite and personal hygiene habits and a life span of average length. The only drawback is that the ibex is sensitive to large crowds; given the exhibit's popularity, this may lead to problems. Design and place this exhibit thoughtfully.

The ibex does not play a prescribed role in any of the game's scenarios; nevertheless, you'll generally want to adopt it when it is available and you have the right money.

AMERICAN BIGHORN SHEEP

Attractiveness: 15/45

Minimum cost: $1,800

Animals in exhibit/shelter: 3–10, lean-to

Manageability: Average

Exhibit type and size: North American highlands, 20 tiles per animal, 50% suitability

Habitat: 70% brown rock, 20% gray rock, 5% grass, 5% fresh water; 7% rocks, 3% foliage—paper birch, western larch

Comments: The American bighorn is a solid choice. This amiable animal adapts flexibly to both captivity and its habitat, and the large area of brown rock required makes it possible to utilize the existing features of many maps. This animal is an accomplished eater and a modest poo producer; it reproduces easily, and if its slightly shaky health is cared for it lives to a grand old age. It also doesn't mind crowds much.

Although this species does not play a major prescribed role in any of the set scenarios, it might help you meet the winning conditions of at least one. Acquiring this species is almost always a safe, profitable move. If money's a little tight, the bighorn is an excellent choice for your first highland species exhibit.

POLAR ANIMALS

This group consists of three species native to Earth's northern and southern extremes: the Arctic and the Antarctic. All of them score highly in terms of attractiveness, and one (the polar bear) is a good choice if money's tight.

POLAR BEAR

Attractiveness: 50/150

Minimum cost: $1,500

Animals in exhibit/shelter: 1–3, snowy rock cave

Manageability: Average

Exhibit type and size: Polar (Arctic), 35 tiles per animal, 70% suitability

Habitat: 50% snow, 50% salt water; 4% rocks, 0% foliage

Comments: The ease of building the perfect polar bear habitat offsets this animal's slightly troublesome traits: It doesn't like captivity or big crowds and is a voracious eater with a digestion to match. The polar bear has surprisingly shaky health, but if cared for well will live a long life. Getting it to reproduce may be slightly difficult; make sure it has enough privacy.

　　The polar bear does not star in any scenarios, but the acquisition of a single animal of this species is frequently a wise move in a freeform game, particularly if money is tight.

ARCTIC WOLF

Attractiveness: 15/45

Minimum cost: $4,600

Animals in exhibit/shelter: 4–20, snowy rock cave

Manageability: Average

Exhibit type and size: Arctic, 35 tiles per animal, 85% suitability

Habitat: 80% snow, 15% grey rock, 5% fresh water; 8% rocks, 0% foliage

Comments: The Arctic wolf is a pretty expensive choice, but its exhibit may become one of the most popular in your zoo. This animal's needs require you to construct a very large exhibit. It has a short life span, though that is of little consequence; creating a good habitat is invariably rewarded with plenty of wolf puppies. Arctic wolves have a good appetite, but are fairly clean—keeping the exhibit tidy isn't very difficult even given a large number of animals. They display average crowd sensitivity, but initially are fairly unhappy; it is important to quickly provide them with the ideal habitat.

　　The Arctic wolf does not play a prescribed star role in any scenario. However, an exhibit containing a happy pack of these animals is a huge attraction; make sure they feel comfortable and can hide from sight.

EMPEROR PENGUIN

Attractiveness: 15/45

Minimum cost: $2,200

Animals in exhibit/shelter: 2–16, snowy rock cave

Manageability: Average

Exhibit type and size: Polar (Antarctic), 15 tiles per animal, 70% suitability

Habitat: 60% salt water, 40% snow; 6% rocks, 0% foliage

Comments: This bird is another polar winner—a big emperor penguin exhibit ranks as a top attraction. What's more, this animal displays agreeable characteristics that make them reasonably easy to care for (of course, the difficulty increases with the number of animals). It is a restrained eater and poo producer, takes well to captivity, doesn't mind crowds, and enjoys good health. It doesn't live long, but given its fairly easy reproduction this isn't a problem.

The penguin doesn't star in any scenarios. Nevertheless, it's a good choice in almost all games of *Zoo Tycoon*. Its exhibit works out pretty cheaply in terms of attractiveness, especially since no strong barriers are needed.

DESERT ANIMALS

The hardy species in this group include the gemsbok and the dromedary camel. Both animals have the potential to attract numerous guests, though neither can be really called a zoo star.

GEMSBOK

Attractiveness: 10/30

Minimum cost: $2,700

Animals in exhibit/shelter: 3–15, stable

Manageability: Easy

Exhibit type and size: African desert, 20 tiles per animal, 60% suitability

Habitat: 70% sand, 15% savannah grass, 10% dirt, 5% fresh water; 2% rocks, 3% foliage—quiver tree, prickly pear cactus, palm tree

Comments: This antelope is a solid choice even when you're not planning a desert-themed mini-area. It enjoys very good health that lets it live out an average life span, doesn't mind captivity or crowds much, and reproduces fairly easily. It does have an appetite and poo-making talents that equal the lion's, but this is not a meaningful drawback given the other advantages.

The gemsbok is highlighted in one of the game's set scenarios. It is a solid choice in a freeform game, providing a respectable return on the required investment.

Dromedary Camel

Attractiveness: 10/30

Minimum cost: $900

Animals in exhibit/shelter: 1–10, stable

Manageability: Easy

Exhibit type and size: African desert, 20 tiles per animal, 90% suitability

Habitat: 88% sand, 10% dirt, 2% fresh water; 1% rocks, 1% foliage—quiver tree, prickly pear cactus, palm tree

Comments: The dromedary camel is a safe, if not very exciting, choice in most situations. Crowds and captivity don't bother it much, and it has a hearty appetite with appropriate poo-making ability. The camel is somewhat exacting in its habitat requirements, but once these are met it reproduces fairly easily. Its health is not as strong as you might expect; you must care for it well to enable it to live out its average life span.

This species is highlighted in one of the early scenarios. It's usually a solid choice in freeform games; its exhibit is relatively inexpensive.

Saltwater Animals

Zoo Tycoon also features two species of aquatic animals: the saltwater crocodile and the California sea lion. Both are popular with the zoo public, the sea lion especially—its exhibit is bound to become one of your zoo's hot spots.

Saltwater Crocodile

Attractiveness: 60/120

Minimum cost: $3,000

Animals in exhibit/shelter: 2–3, none

Manageability: Average

Exhibit type and size: Sea shore, 20 tiles per animal, 70% suitability

Habitat: 80% salt water, 20% dirt; 2% rocks, 8% foliage—water reed

Comments: This animal's exhibit is made cheaper by the fact it requires only low (though strong) barriers. Given its relatively low cost and high attractiveness, it's a very good choice. Saltwater crocodiles aren't difficult to care for; the biggest problem tends to be the amount of poo they produce (they have good appetites). Also, they display a small amount of crowd sensitivity; if they fail to reproduce, usually crowds are to blame. It's very easy to make their habitat fully meet their requirements; just remember to provide these animals with some privacy. They enjoy average health and an average life span.

Crocodiles are prominently featured in one of the game's earlier scenarios and are almost invariably a good acquisition in a freeform game.

California Sea Lion

Attractiveness: 20/60

Minimum cost: $1,400

Animals in exhibit/shelter: 2–16, none

Manageability: Somewhat difficult

Exhibit type and size: Sea shore, 35 tiles per animal, 70% suitability

Habitat: 90% salt water, 10% gray rock; 0% rocks, 0% foliage

Comments: This animal is everybody's favorite! A big sea lion exhibit is a star attraction; when planning it, remember to provide some privacy for the animals. (Even animals fairly tolerant of crowds have their limits!) It's probably best to assign a dedicated zookeeper, because sea lions eat a lot and make a lot of poo. They adapt well to captivity and enjoy very good health; unfortunately, they have a short life span. Reproduction isn't difficult if enough privacy is provided.

Sea lions star in a later scenario, and they are a very good addition to every zoo. However, to capitalize on their attraction potential, you have to save up enough cash to shell out for a really big exhibit.

Mystery Animals

In addition to the animals described previously, *Zoo Tycoon* features two secret species that will be yours to enjoy once you've completed the final two scenarios. Completing "Paradise Island Zoo" releases Mystery Beast #1; completing "Breed the Giant Pandas" unleashes Mystery Beast #2. Both mystery species are thereafter available in every *Zoo Tycoon* game you play.

In addition to these two, a third Mystery Beast is to be released to *Zoo Tycoon* owners by Internet download a short time after the release of the game.

Mystery Beast #1

Attractiveness: 90/270

Minimum cost: $12,000

Animals in exhibit/shelter: 2–4, lean-to

Manageability: Difficult

Exhibit type and size: Deciduous forest, 60 tiles per animal, 80% suitability

Habitat: 80% deciduous forest, 10% grass, 10% fresh water; 4% rocks, 15% foliage—Japanese maple tree, cherry, maple

Comments: You've undoubtedly seen one sometime during the past few months…yet there are none kicking around. Both ancient and modern books frequently talk about it…enough said.

This unique animal becomes available when you complete "Paradise Island Zoo." Although it's by no means tiny, it eats like a weight-conscious mouse, producing hardly any poo. It's shy, but its amiable nature doesn't allow it to dislike captivity or people to a large degree. Unfortunately, its health is extremely delicate, and even given the best care it has a short life span. Getting it to reproduce is very difficult.

This animal's phenomenal attractiveness justifies building more than one exhibit containing it. Not cheap—but the return's more than worth it.

MYSTERY BEAST #2

Attractiveness: 95/285

Minimum cost: $20,000

Animals in exhibit/shelter: 2–10, none

Manageability: Very difficult

Exhibit type and size: Savannah, 50 tiles per animal, 85% suitability

Habitat: 75% savannah grass, 15% dirt, 5% sand, 5% fresh water; 2% rocks, 9% foliage—grass tree, thorn bush

Comments: The fact that this species likes both the grass tree and the thorn bush is a hint. Again, you're sure to have seen this animal at some point in time; it starred in a prominent movie not that long ago. It may very well be the biggest animal in your zoo when you acquire it—it can certainly compete with any pachyderms you've got…enough clues.

This animal, which becomes available after you complete the game's final scenario, is certainly a lot of trouble. Feeding it and getting rid of the resulting poo is a major task and so is keeping it healthy—it is extremely sickly, particularly considering its size. Taken good care of, it can live a long life, but getting it to reproduce is extremely difficult; it's a question of timing, you might say. This beast is reasonably tolerant of crowds, but dislikes captivity. You'll greatly improve the chances of its happy existence if you assign dedicated zookeepers—yes, you might need more than one for several animals of this species.

Mystery Beast #2 is the biggest zoo attraction in *Zoo Tycoon*.

CHAPTER 4

THE ZOO PEOPLE

A ZOO DOESN'T CONSIST SOLELY OF ANIMALS; THERE ARE ALSO SEVERAL TYPES OF HUMAN BEINGS WHOSE ACTIONS ARE ESSENTIAL TO THE ZOO'S SURVIVAL AND SUCCESS. ZOOKEEPERS AND MAINTENANCE WORKERS ARE ESSENTIAL ZOO STAFF WITHOUT WHOM YOUR ENTERPRISE FACES QUICK COLLAPSE, WHILE TOUR GUIDES HELP KEEP ZOO GUESTS HAPPY BY INFORMING THEM ABOUT THE ANIMAL SPECIES REPRESENTED IN YOUR ZOO. NATURALLY, ZOO GUESTS CONSTITUTE THE LIFEBLOOD OF YOUR BUSINESS. YOU CAN EXPECT TO BE BAILED OUT OF FINANCIAL TROUBLE ONLY ONCE (SEE CHAPTER 7); AFTER THAT, YOUR SUCCESS DEPENDS ON THE ZOO GUESTS AND THEIR VOLUMINOUS POCKETS. YOU'LL BE HAPPY TO KNOW THAT THE ZOO GUESTS ARE A VERY WELL HEELED CROWD!

YOU'LL BE ABLE TO WATCH ZOO GUESTS AND STAFF ON YOUR GAME SCREEN. HOWEVER, THERE IS ALSO ANOTHER CATEGORY OF PEOPLE IN THE GAME. THESE PEOPLE ARE INVISIBLE; THEIR ACTIVITIES TAKE PLACE BEHIND THE SCENES, YET THEY ARE OF CRUCIAL IMPORTANCE TO YOU AND YOUR ZOO. THIS CHAPTER DISCUSSES ALL THE PEOPLE IN THE GAME—BOTH VISIBLE AND INVISIBLE—AND THEIR ROLES IN YOUR SUCCESS.

ZOO STAFF

There are three categories of zoo employees: zookeepers, maintenance workers, and tour guides. Each type of employee performs certain specialized functions within your zoo. Employee wages are a significant item in the zoo budget, and any hiring decisions you make should be well thought out. The following sections, which examine zoo staff in detail, should give you a good idea what to expect.

ZOOKEEPERS

Zookeepers are the only absolutely essential staff (see Figure 4.1). A zoo can survive without any of the guest amenities that necessitate trashcans, and you can elect to do any fence repairs yourself. This means you can get by without maintenance workers; a zoo can also survive happily without a single tour guide. But a zoo must have at least one animal on exhibit to exist at all, and an animal cannot survive without a zookeeper.

FIGURE 4.1:

This guy in the cool brown hat is your single most important employee.

Zookeepers perform four important tasks, which are listed here in descending order of priority:

1 They subdue escaped animals. When an animal escapes through a fence that's deteriorated or broken down, the nearest zookeeper drops everything and gets out the dart gun. The tranquilized animal is put in a transport container with the zookeeper waiting alongside; you have to pick up the container and put it inside the appropriate exhibit before the valiant zookeeper returns to his interrupted duties. Remember to repair that fence!

2 They feed the animals. This is the first thing zookeepers do upon arriving in an exhibit; they'll do it even when they're picked up and placed in an exhibit to help a sick animal. Call it insurance against getting eaten.

3 They heal sick animals. This is the second task every zookeeper performs automatically upon entering or being placed in an exhibit. If there are any sick animals in the exhibit, you'll see a white medical bag pop out and hear the reassuring tinkling of tiny bells. If there are no sick animals in the exhibit, the zookeeper automatically will move on to item number four on this list.

4 They clean up animal poo. This thankless task is always last in priority; if large amounts of poo cause a sudden drop in exhibit suitability near the end of a scenario, you could be in trouble. Better place two zookeepers in the affected exhibit right away!

TIP

Always try to hire any new zoo staff as early in the month as possible. Even if you hire an employee on the last day of the month, you'll still have to pay them a full month's salary.

Zookeepers are very expensive: they collect $800 the moment they're hired and again on the first day of every subsequent month.

The number of exhibits that can be successfully serviced by one zookeeper varies greatly. A lot rides on the size and number of animals inside the exhibit (bigger animals tend to produce more poo). The distances your zookeeper has to walk also play a role; good placement of exhibit gates is very important.

Zookeepers can be assigned to specific exhibits, or they can operate in a freelance mode, monitoring the zoo and entering exhibits that need servicing. You'll want to consider assigning zookeepers to specific exhibits; for one thing, it allows you to adjust the placement of exhibit gates for maximum efficiency. Also, a zookeeper assigned to an exhibit will enter that exhibit more frequently, each appearance giving the animals inside a happiness boost. Big, busy zoos also benefit from the presence of a few freelance zookeepers.

On the average, you'll find that a zookeeper is capable of handling up to 10 animals as long as he can move between exhibits in an efficient manner. A huge exhibit, such as the mixed African savannah, requires its own dedicated zookeeper. Keep in mind that happy animals reproduce, swelling the exhibit population—a zookeeper who has been successfully handling three exhibits may suddenly find it difficult to take care of two!

You can make your zookeepers more efficient by researching the relevant staff education programs: Zookeeper Training 1, Zookeeper Training 2, and Panda Enrichment. This last program is featured only in the last scenario ("Breeding Giant Pandas"). Please refer to Chapter 5 for more details.

Maintenance Workers

Most of your maintenance workers' duties revolve around trash and dirt. Their pay reflects this sad status: It's only $300 a month. This instantly makes maintenance workers an excellent value, since they do perform one valuable duty that does not involve trash: They repair exhibit fencing. When you consider that a single section of concrete wall fencing can cost up to $200, it's obvious that each maintenance worker is worth his weight in gold (perhaps that's why they wear shiny yellow hardhats). All it takes is a few taps with a hammer, and a deteriorated fencing section is as good as new.

There is no sequence set in stone in which your maintenance workers move to their next job. They like to finish what they've started, and so a maintenance worker sweeping up trash is not likely to interrupt this task as long as there's trash littering the ground nearby. However, idle maintenance workers tend to follow this sequence when suddenly faced with a variety of tasks:

1   They make up their minds what to do next. This is important because maintenance workers feel a strong common bond and like to do things as a team. It may happen that all of them decide that emptying a particular trashcan is priority number one. As the manager of the zoo, you must keep a close watch on the thought processes of your maintenance workers by checking their information panels, which display the task they intend to do next. Fight their herd instinct by picking them up and

placing them as far apart as possible. In short, you must behave like a real zoo manager, walking around and telling people where they should get their body parts to work.

2 As a rule, repairing damaged fencing is the next priority. As mentioned, this is where maintenance workers really earn their keep.

3 Full trashcans and trash lying on the ground come next. Maintenance workers come equipped with an unlimited supply of black garbage bags that are used on these occasions and subsequently disappear with a mysterious rustle.

This second point should convince you that there's very little point in trying to save money by scrimping on maintenance workers. You should definitely have one per 50 zoo guests, and preferably more. Note that you can improve maintenance worker efficiency by researching the relevant staff education programs: Maintenance Worker 1 and 2. See Chapter 5 for details.

Tour Guides

Tour guides make zoo guests gathered in observation areas happier by 10%. Their eloquence comes at a considerable cost—$500 a month—and this instantly makes tour guides something of a superfluous luxury in small and many medium-sized zoos. However, once your zoo grows to a really big size (20 exhibits or more), you may find yourself fighting to prevent average guest happiness from slipping. By that time, you'll also be able to afford tour guides.

Note that tour guides may be assigned to specific exhibits, just like zookeepers. You'll achieve a good cost/efficiency ratio if you assign each tour guide to a specific theme area or three to four exhibits, whichever comes first. When tour guides aren't assigned to any exhibits, they tend to stay in a defined area anyway, moving back and forth between adjacent exhibits. In the later stages of the game, you should consider investing in staff education to research Tour Guide Training 1 (see Chapter 5 for details).

Zoo Guests

Guests are the people who will make or break your zoo. Understanding where they come from, what makes them happy, and what makes them spend money is essential for every aspiring tycoon. The sections that follow describe a guest's journey through your zoo, with special emphasis on happiness and money (no, they're not the same thing).

WHY THEY COME

The number of people who are willing to pay good money to see your zoo depends on a combination of two factors: zoo rating and admission price. The game features three zoo rating thresholds and four admission price thresholds. These are as follows:

- **Zoo rating:** Over 80, between 30 and 80, and under 30

- **Admission price:** Very expensive ($49+), expensive ($29.25–$49), normal ($19.25–$29), cheap ($9.25–$19), and free. Setting the price to expensive means very few guests will appear, if any (see Figure 4.2).

FIGURE 4.2:

The admission price may be used as a filter to determine the number of guests in your zoo.

The combination of zoo rating and admission price yields a specific chance (high: 30%, medium: 25%, low: 5%, very low: 3%) of a new guest showing up at the zoo gates. Naturally, high zoo rating and free or cheap admission maximize the chance of new guests appearing at the entrance, while a very poor zoo charging a steep admission price will hardly ever see any. See Chapter 7 for further advice on setting the admission price.

WHO THEY ARE

Each new zoo guest has a randomly designated sex, age, and favorite animal. You can find out a guest's favorite animal from the Guest Information panel; naturally, their sex and age are evident on the game screen. Also, you should note that every guest has randomly generated happiness, hunger, thirst, energy, and restroom need levels. You'll repeatedly see guests entering the zoo and throwing themselves right at a food stand before they as much as glance at an animal.

A guest's sex and age are very important: they determine the guest's aesthetic preferences and the amount of happiness they feel in any given set of circumstances. Appendices B and C contain relevant numerical data; the following section discusses general guest happiness issues.

WHY THEY STAY

Guests will stay longer in your zoo if they like it there—it's that simple. Since the longer they stay, the more money they spend, prolonging their visit is in your best interest. You can have guests happily spend whole months in your zoo by meeting all of their needs and providing attractions that make them happy.

The Guest List button is a great tool for keeping tabs on your guests—you instantly know how many guests there are in your zoo, and also how many are hungry, thirsty, tired, or in need of a restroom. Satisfying these needs (all of which are represented by colored bars on the Guest Information panel) increases guest happiness (top bar on the Guest Info panel). Guests whose needs aren't met for a long time eventually become angry (if they haven't left the zoo in the meantime). Angry guests mean a decrease in zoo rating, which may start a whole chain reaction of unpleasant events, or even lose you a scenario game.

When a bar representing a guest need turns red, the guest concerned feels a wave of unhappiness. The size of the resulting decrease in happiness level ranges from –10 (the guest is tired or cannot find a souvenir) through –20 (the guest is hungry or thirsty) to –30 (the guest needs to use a restroom *right now*).

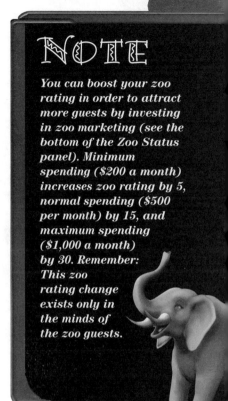

NOTE

You can boost your zoo rating in order to attract more guests by investing in zoo marketing (see the bottom of the Zoo Status panel). Minimum spending ($200 a month) increases zoo rating by 5, normal spending ($500 per month) by 15, and maximum spending ($1,000 a month) by 30. Remember: This zoo rating change exists only in the minds of the zoo guests.

SIMPLE PLEASURES

Satisfying a guest's needs, logically enough, often increases their happiness. Appendix B has the specific numerical values, listing the increases in happiness guests derive from purchasing and eating food, using the restroom (a whopping +20 boost from the deluxe family model!), and so on. An adult who loves hamburgers will be practically swooning with pleasure upon getting to a burger shack, getting a basic +10 boost from buying the burger and another +30 from eating it (+20 basic bonus, +10 preferred food bonus).

The prices you charge for the items sold in your zoo can have an effect ranging from a +15 increase to a –25 decrease in guest happiness. Naturally, the actual change depends on how happy a guest is in the first place; a very happy guest pays top dollar without a negative thought, and normal pricing can even provide a small happiness boost. Check Chapter 7 for details.

> **NOTE**
>
> When the percentage of hungry, tired, thirsty, or otherwise displeased guests in your zoo reaches a significant level, you'll see an appropriate warning message (e.g. "There are many hungry guests"). Unfortunately, its appearance is linked to a decrease in zoo rating.

FIGURE 4.3:
"I'm daaaancing in the rain...."

In addition to meeting guest needs, you must also provide a sufficient number of attractions. These include both happy animals and certain zoo buildings; happy animals are naturally far more important.

THE ANIMALS

Guests get a tremendous kick out of seeing happy animals; this single benefit can keep them happy even when they're tired, hungry, or whatnot. A guest viewing an exhibit with a "very happy" rating (one with an average animal happiness score over 81) receives a +10 happiness bonus; any baby animals provide another +10 boost. An exhibit with multiple animal species increases guest happiness by +5, while seeing a favorite animal provides a happiness boost of +30.

Unhappy and/or sick animals make guests feel bad. Every sick animal viewed by a guest decreases their happiness by –20, while every unhappy animal decreases it by –10 to –35 (depending on the degree of unhappiness existing on both sides).

> ## NOTE
>
> *Ideally, the bars on the Guest Info panel should be green at all times. However, in a well-designed zoo, a guest who is somewhat hungry, thirsty, tired, and in need of a bathroom (yellow bars) can still be 100% happy. In an excellent zoo, a guest may continue feeling happy even when a bar in the Guest Info panel turns red (see Figure 4.3).*

THE ATTRACTIONS

An animal theater, a Japanese garden, an elephant ride, a carousel, and an animal house are all examples of zoo buildings that count as zoo attractions. All of the attractions are listed in Appendix B, but here are the main points:

- Some attractions make you money and others don't, but all provide guest happiness boosts (see Appendix B). These boosts often vary depending on the sex and age of the guest and in certain cases may apply only to a specific age group. You'll also find more on the subject in Chapters 5 and 6. Note that only moneymaking attractions incur upkeep costs (animal houses with advanced exhibits are exceptions; see Chapter 5).

- Selected attractions (such as the animal theater and carousel) are such good moneymakers that they remain profitable even when you slash prices to the bone, thus giving guests yet another happiness boost.

🖐 Numerous attractions *cannot* make up for a low number of animal exhibits/species represented in your zoo. A good ratio of attractions to exhibits is 1 to 1.

🖐 Careful placement of attractions can be very helpful in managing the flow of zoo traffic. Putting the entrance to an attraction a few tiles to the side of a main path can induce many guests to walk down the side path, reducing congestion on main zoo routes.

Moneymaking attractions assume special importance in scenario games, where they are all available right at the start of the game; they can be of major assistance in funding an intense effort to meet scenario goals. In freeform games, you'll be forced to wait a while before any attractions become available—see Chapter 5 for details.

THE BEAUTY

Guests like beauty. Every single visitor to your zoo expects things to be up to a certain aesthetic standard. Satisfying this standard instantly results in a +10 boost to guest happiness.

Of course, if your zoo is strewn with trash, things turn ugly. The presence of four pieces of trash per megatile carries an instant –10 hit to guest happiness (accompanied by the guest thought, "This zoo is dirty."). This is irrespective of any effect the trash has on the megatile's aesthetic value: four pieces of trash equal an aesthetic hit of –60. Note that trashcans—whether empty or overflowing—are hardly any prettier: They carry a –10 aesthetic hit.

Since your zoo's beauty also has an influence on zoo rating (see Chapter 6), you should pay due attention to zoo aesthetics. Simple remedies such as keeping your zoo trash free work wonders; a nice-looking path lined with decorative fencing (see Figure 4.4) is the first step to make guests happy with your zoo's beauty. See Chapter 6 for some extra advice in this area, and use Appendix C to keep track of the aesthetics of your zoo.

FIGURE 4.4:

Basic beauty works best.

THE INVISIBLE ONES

There are two more categories of people in *Zoo Tycoon*, and one of them is of absolutely crucial importance. You won't see any of these people on your game screen, but you'll feel their presence (or their absence!) pretty sharply. Well, enough of the mystery: These people are the benefactors of your zoo and the protesters who take to the streets when you have many sick animals in your zoo.

ZOO BENEFACTORS

You don't get to deal with them, but your accountant does, and that's all that matters. The Zoo Status panel lists the number of zoo benefactors who are currently writing you checks on the first day of the month. Unfortunately, zoo benefactors' enthusiasm tends to be short-lived, and you must constantly find new ones in order to keep the green stuff coming in.

Every really happy guest (over 80 happiness) who leaves your zoo has a chance of becoming a zoo benefactor; more happy guests mean more potential benefactors. When the new month rolls around, each new benefactor writes out a check for between $100 and $300 (the actual amount is random). This does not go on forever; upon pulling out the old checkbook a month later, the benefactor may experience a change of mind and disappear. The chance of this happening is determined by your current zoo rating; a lower rating results in more disappearing benefactors.

PROTESTERS

The presence of protesters is announced by an angry red message on the game screen. Although you'll never see any protesters on the game screen, their presence is a very loud alarm bell that signals great neglect of the animals in your zoo. Although the animals that remain healthy may be very happy, the number of sick animals on display causes a wave of sadness to pass through your guests and brings a significant decrease in zoo rating. You have to be very lax for any of this to happen; since you have this book, it won't happen. Enough said.

ZOO EVOLUTION

ASUCCESSFUL ZOO IS A ZOO THAT'S UNDERGOING CONSTANT CHANGE. THIS QUALITY IS PARTICULARLY STRESSED IN THE SCENARIOS, ALL OF WHICH SET A TIGHT TIME LIMIT ON ACHIEVING UP TO 12 WINNING CONDITIONS (MOST COMMONLY, AROUND HALF A DOZEN).

A LOT OF THE CHANGES ARE POSSIBLE ONLY AFTER YOU'VE COMPLETED APPROPRIATE RESEARCH. THERE ARE MANY SCENARIOS THAT YOU CANNOT COMPLETE WITHOUT ACHIEVING SEVERAL ADVANCED RESEARCH OBJECTIVES THAT BELONG TO DIFFERENT RESEARCH FIELDS. WHEN PLAYING A FREEFORM GAME, YOU WON'T FACE THAT KIND OF PRESSURE—YOU'LL BE ALLOWED TO CONDUCT RESEARCH AT YOUR OWN PACE—BUT YOU'LL ALSO HAVE TO WAIT A YEAR BEFORE ALL OF THE GAME'S STANDARD STRUCTURES AND ANIMALS BECOME AVAILABLE. THIS MAY SEVERELY CRAMP YOUR STYLE AT THE OUTSET, ESPECIALLY SINCE THE BIG MONEYMAKING ATTRACTIONS BECOME AVAILABLE ONLY AT THE END OF YOUR FIRST YEAR IN BUSINESS. THIS CHAPTER WILL DISCUSS ZOO EVOLUTION IN ALL ITS FORMS, HOPEFULLY HELPING YOU MUTATE INTO A NEW AND IMPROVED TYCOON.

RESEARCH AND CONSERVATION

Zoo Tycoon features two areas of research: Research and Conservation. These are subdivided into seven different fields, each of which contains up to 10 specific objectives. This section lists all of them in the order established in the game. It also includes the extra Panda Care Research category, which is available only in *Zoo Tycoon*'s final scenario ("Breeding Giant Pandas").

RESEARCH

This area consists of four fields: Animal Shelters, Staff Education, Animal Care, and Animal Enrichment. This is the order in which they appear on the Research panel, but their relative importance differs from scenario to scenario, depending on the specific winning conditions.

> ### NOTE
>
> *Scenario games often require a very focused effort in one or more fields at the expense of the others; you'll find details in Chapter 8. Also, you don't choose the research sequence in any field. In some fields, the sequence in which objectives are researched is determined at random; other fields feature a set sequence (see the following sections).*

Unsurprisingly, you should begin by researching Animal Care (or at least its first two programs). In freeform games, it often makes sense to follow with Animal Enrichment, which deals with animal toys. Putting a toy into an exhibit lets you tweak its suitability to the point where you could collect the Gold Plaque for Excellence in Exhibit Design—an award that's accompanied by $15,000 (see Chapter 6). Research the remaining parts of Animal Care or the first two levels of Staff Education next, leaving Animal Shelters until the very end; new types of shelters are made available throughout the first year of a freeform game anyway.

Zoo Tycoon's final scenario culminates in the birth of a baby panda; to this end, it features an extra, scenario-specific Research category called Panda Care. Researching the three programs available under Panda Care is, of course, a prerequisite to winning the scenario.

ANIMAL SHELTERS

As previously explained, this field should generally be researched *last*. The new kinds of shelters you'll get through research aren't much more than family-size versions of the ones you already have; however, you should remember that a large shelter of any kind always works much better than two small shelters of the same kind (see Figure 5.1). Animals appreciate extra room and are particularly happy if you're able to provide them with the kind of shelter they like most; the game provides relevant info. Some species (e.g., the panda) are so picky that they may need a special shelter before they'll be happy enough to reproduce. However, most species do well given a concrete shelter, with the large concrete shelter (which must be researched) being a particularly good all-around performer.

FIGURE 5.1:

Remember that one big shelter is always better than two smaller ones; upgrade exhibits as new shelter types become available.

Shelters are researched in a random sequence, meaning that you could begin with the Rock Cave in one game and with the Large Concrete Shelter in another. Bearing this in mind, here are the types of shelter that can be researched:

- **Large Burrow:** Burrows are available without any research; however, this is the top-of-the-line, deluxe model loved by anteaters and warthogs.

- **Large Concrete Shelter:** When in doubt, build a Large Concrete Shelter. It's the second-best choice for almost all of the species in the game.

- **Large Elephant Shelter:** This is another species-specific shelter that's a bigger, better version of the shelter that's otherwise available.

- *Ⓒ* **Large Giraffe Shelter:** As the name indicates, this type of shelter is used by giraffes only. A small giraffe shelter is available without research, but it doesn't work as well.

- *Ⓒ* **Large Lean-to:** Especially favored by okapi and non-carnivorous highland animals (ibex, markhorn, American bighorn sheep). Also a big favorite with a mystery beast native to deep deciduous forests, and the right choice for smaller hoofed animals from the savannah (gazelle, zebra, wildebeest) as well as the ostrich.

- *Ⓒ* **Large Stable:** This is a firm favorite with many large hoofed quadrupeds of savannah, grassland, and desert species: African buffalo, American bison, camel, and gemsbok.

- *Ⓒ* **Large Wood Shelter:** This shelter is the equivalent of the Large Concrete Shelter for many species. It's an acceptable substitute for rainforest, savannah, deciduous, and coniferous forest animals.

- *Ⓒ* **Panda Cave:** The name says it all. Pandas won't reproduce without one.

- *Ⓒ* **Rock Cave:** This is the preferred shelter of coniferous forest species (grizzly, gray wolf, Siberian tiger) and the rainforest cats (tigers, black and clouded leopards, jaguar). It's also a favorite with the black bear.

- *Ⓒ* **Snowy Rock Cave:** This is a favorite with polar species (polar bear, arctic wolf, emperor penguin) as well as with the snow leopard.

STAFF EDUCATION

This field contains two objectives that you should research immediately after Animal Care: Zookeeper Training 1 and Maintenance Worker Training 1 (see Figure 5.2). There's a random element involved in the sequence; however, all level 1 staff education programs (including Tour Guide Training 1) must be completed before you can research level 2 programs. Note that there is no level 2 training for tour guides.

- *Ⓒ* **Maintenance Worker Training 1:** This training enables your maintenance workers to perform 25% more efficiently when sweeping up trash. There's no heavier hit to zoo beauty than trash lying on the ground, so dealing with it quickly is important.

- **Zookeeper Training 1:** Upon completing this program, zookeepers give animals an extra 10% happiness bonus when they enter an exhibit. Animal happiness is the single most important consideration in running your zoo, so Zookeeper Training 1 is extremely useful.

- **Tour Guide Training 1:** After training, tour guides can make zoo guests 10% happier than they could previously. This is an important skill; however, zoo finances frequently won't permit you to hire tour guides while proceeding with dynamic zoo expansion. This program is best completed when there are no other research priorities.

- **Maintenance Worker Training 2:** This training enables your maintenance workers to get better at repairing fences. This is useful in proportion to the size of your zoo and the number of exhibits therein, but obviously isn't of burning importance.

- **Zookeeper Training 2:** This program allows your zookeepers to move 25% faster. This results in improving zookeeper efficiency all around and is of particular importance in larger zoos.

FIGURE 5.2:

Basic zookeeper and maintenance worker training makes a significant difference in busier zoos.

ANIMAL CARE

There are four Research objectives in this field, and they're researched in the following order.

1 **Nutritional Food:** In practice, completing this program means that animals can be fed 25% less often at the same cost (which means it costs you 25% less over time).

2 **Animal Fertility:** In terms of research priorities, this is the mother of all programs. Higher animal fertility means more babies, which in turn mean great boosts in exhibit attractiveness, more happiness all around, and income from animal sales.

3 **Reduced Food Costs:** This program is not very important in itself, but you must complete it in order to research Animal Antibiotics, which *are* important. The 10% reduction in feeding costs that results from completing this program does add up to quite a few bucks in a big zoo, but a big zoo makes so much money that the difference is hardly noticeable.

4 **Animal Antibiotics:** This is *Zoo Tycoon*'s take on veterinary vaccines; completing this program reduces the likelihood of sickness among your animals by 10%. This makes a big zoo more manageable and the gameplay more pleasant (there are many fewer warning messages to interrupt important tycoon activity).

TIP

Nutritional Food and Animal Fertility are very high research priorities in any game of Zoo Tycoon, scenario or freeform.

ANIMAL ENRICHMENT

This category includes five types of animal toys. Animal toys play an important part in raising both animal happiness and habitat suitability, one independently of the other. A random element is involved in the research order: Most often you'll start with the Swinging Log Toy or Large Lion Climbing Rock, followed by either Large Chimpanzee Bars or Gorilla Climbing Bars, and ending with the Cat Climbing Tree.

🐾 **Swinging Log Toy:** This toy is very useful in keeping elephants happy.

🐾 **Lion Climbing Rock:** Practically all zoos have a lion exhibit; it's arguably the best choice for starting a freeform zoo. This toy usually inspires your lions to reproduce as long as the habitat's well appointed.

- **Large Chimpanzee Bars:** This toy is better at keeping chimps happy than the small chimpanzee bars available without any research. It's not a must-have, though.

- **Gorilla Climbing Bars:** You'd be well advised to research this animal toy before you adopt a lowland gorilla for your zoo. Gorillas are very moody animals; these climbing bars are often just what's needed to keep their spirits from deteriorating.

- **Cat Climbing Tree:** Shy, sensitive leopards feel much better when they have this toy. It makes captivity more cheerful for leopards from the African savannah and for the clouded and black varieties; snow leopards couldn't care less.

PANDA CARE

This specialized field contains three Research objectives, which are always researched in the order presented in the following list. Note that keeping a panda happy also involves researching the appropriate exhibit foliage (bamboo) and animal shelter (panda cave).

1. **Panda Enrichment:** Completing this Research program results in a 10% boost to panda happiness. Very useful, as pandas are rather unhappy by nature.

2. **Panda Inoculations:** Developing a special panda vaccine reduces the risk of illness by 25% for these animals.

3. **Panda Fertility:** You don't have much of a chance of breeding pandas without completing this Research program.

> **NOTE**
>
> *Animal Houses aren't highlighted by any of the scenarios; at the same time, they count as zoo attractions and work hard at raising average guest happiness level in exchange for a modest investment.*

CONSERVATION

Conservation covers three fields: Endangered Animals, Animal Houses, and Exhibit Foliage. Research priorities vary greatly depending on whether you're playing a set scenario or a freeform game. When playing scenarios, you'll most likely research Endangered Animals first and Exhibit Foliage second, with Animal Houses at the very end. When playing a freeform game, it pays to research these fields in exactly the opposite sequence: Animal Houses (at the very least the initial set of four programs) first, then Exhibit Foliage, and finally Endangered Animals.

Endangered Animals

Endangered species figure largely in many of the scenarios; winning conditions in one scenario or another include researching, adopting, and/or breeding all but one of the six species in this category (lowland gorillas). Getting these high-strung, sensitive animals to reproduce can be extremely difficult (which is exactly why they're endangered as a species—see Figure 5.3).

FIGURE 5.3:
Will they or won't they? The difficulty of getting certain animals to reproduce may lead to nail-biting suspense when a scenario deadline draws near.

Endangered species are researched in a semi-random order: you'll begin with either the white Bengal tiger or the lowland gorilla. After researching these two species, you'll move on to the black leopard, then either the okapi or the snow leopard. Giant pandas are always researched last. All endangered species and their habitat requirements are discussed in more detail in Chapter 3.

1 **Lowland gorilla:** This is the first endangered species to be researched in the vast majority of scenarios and all freeform games. The gorilla is a very demanding animal, and you should also research the appropriate animal toy (gorilla climbing bars) before attempting to adopt any for your zoo.

2   **White Bengal tiger:** This species is highlighted in several scenarios; sometimes, you'll research it before the gorilla. It's relatively easy to care for and does not require extra-specialized research (although a rock cave shelter may be useful in keeping this animal very happy).

3   **Black leopard:** This exotic, rare cat is highlighted in some of the scenarios. It is quite demanding (see Chapter 3); getting it to breed is both a real achievement and a scenario goal ("Endangered Species Zoo").

4   **Snow leopard:** Shy and sensitive, this cat is highlighted in the "Saving the Great Cats" scenario. It requires mountainous terrain and is very finicky about its habitat, which makes building a good exhibit an expensive proposition.

5   **Okapi:** Atypically, this hoofed quadruped inhabits thick African rainforests, not the savannah. It's difficult to care for; scenario goals may include breeding this animal (as in "Endangered Species Zoo").

6   **Giant panda:** The rarest of all endangered species is also the most difficult in terms of animal care. A luxury exhibit and a dedicated zookeeper are both necessary.

Animal Houses

Animal houses are buildings that contain the smaller species of animals (see Figure 5.4). The one-time expenditure involved in building an animal house includes a default exhibit that is free of charge thereafter. You may, however, want to switch the default exhibit (such as Reptiles of the Rainforest) to a more advanced version (such as Deadly Snakes of the World), which gives visiting guests a bigger happiness boost but also incurs monthly upkeep expenses.

None of the animal house exhibits require zookeeper maintenance; all provide guests with happiness boosts independent of the exhibit featured inside. In other words, a zoo guest visiting an animal house usually gets a *double* happiness boost: one from the house itself, the second from the exhibit inside (there are a couple of exceptions, and they are listed further on in this chapter). In addition, animal houses have a positive aesthetic impact, but both the size of that impact and the size of the happiness boost vary from guest to guest.

FIGURE 5.4:

Animal houses are inexpensive attractions that are particularly helpful in maintaining high levels of guest happiness.

Many animal houses, especially the advanced ones, make children especially happy. This is important inasmuch as most zoo structures have a stronger positive effect on adults than they have on children. Child and adult happiness are equally important (many of the guests in your zoo will be children), and animal houses enable you to bring children's happiness up to a level with the adults'.

You'll research the four basic types of animal houses first, but in a random sequence: In some games you'll begin by researching the House of Insects, in others by researching the Aviary, and so on. Once you can build all four types of animal houses (each comes with a default free exhibit), you'll be able to research six advanced animal house exhibits. All animal house research choices are listed in corresponding order below.

Aviary: This house is where the adults get their kicks; children are indifferent to both its presence and its beauty. The Aviary can handle up to 12 guests at any given time. It costs $1,600 and its default exhibit, Birds of the Tropical Rainforest, boosts adult happiness by +5 and child happiness by +3.

TIP

Building a new animal house for each available exhibit helps you push guest happiness up to record levels. You can change the exhibit in a house by clicking on the appropriate icon at the bottom of the House Information panel.

Insect House: This least expensive house holds no joys for adults but big kicks for children; boys think insects look cool, too. There can be only up to four guests in an Insect House at any one time. This house will run you $600; its default exhibit is called Scorpions of Africa and raises adult happiness by +5 and child happiness by +5.

Primate House: This house is a particularly big hit with children, while adults have lukewarm feelings. Both boys and girls think monkeys are beautiful; adults are neutral on the subject. Up to eight guests may visit at any single time. The Primate House costs $1,100 and its default exhibit, Endangered Primates of the World, boosts adult happiness by +5 and child happiness by +3.

Reptile House: Adults find this house mildly attractive; children like it, although not as much as the House of Insects. Boys find special beauty in the slithering inhabitants. This house, which costs $950, can handle up to six guests at a time. The default exhibit is Reptiles of the Rainforest; it provides an adult happiness bonus of +5 and child happiness bonus of +5.

Advanced Animal House Exhibits These become available for research in a semi-random sequence after you complete the four earlier programs. All the second-level exhibits must be researched before either of the two third-level exhibits (5 and 6 in the following list) becomes available for research.

1 Venomous Spiders: This advanced Insect House exhibit incurs $100 per month in upkeep costs. It boosts adult happiness by +8 and child happiness by +12.

2 Deadly Snakes of the World: This is an advanced Reptile House exhibit that requires $120 a month in upkeep. It boosts adult happiness by +10 and child happiness by +12.

3 Primates of Southeast Asia: The first of two advanced Primate House exhibits requires $120 in monthly upkeep. The boost in guest happiness it provides isn't spectacular: Both children and adults get +6.

4 Birds of Africa: The first of two advanced Aviary exhibits; upkeep costs $150 a month. Birds of Africa is a respectable performer that boosts adult happiness by +8 and child happiness by +5.

5 Lemurs of Madagascar: This exhibit only becomes a research option after you've completed the four programs listed previously. It costs $200 a month and is the most attractive Primate House exhibit possible, boosting adult happiness by +10 and child happiness by +15.

6 **Raptors of the World:** This is the other of the two very advanced exhibits that can be researched only after you've completed the first four programs. It costs $200 a month to maintain and is the most attractive choice you can make for an Aviary. Even children are moved by the predatory birds—their happiness boost is +15, which is more than the adults get (+10). However, adults still get a happiness boost from the Aviary itself.

EXHIBIT FOLIAGE

This field contains five research objectives, including the famous bamboo that you need to keep pandas happy. You'll begin your research with either Globe Willow Tree or Thorn Acacia Tree; after this pair is done, the other three foliage types follow in a set order.

1 **Globe Willow Tree:** This is a European deciduous forest tree that's much liked by the game's deciduous forest species.

2 **Thorn Acacia Tree:** This tree from the African savannah is a good second choice for both the warthog and the leopard. It works especially well for leopards; although these cats like baobab trees best, you can fit four thorn acacias into a single tile. This lets you collect a big animal happiness bonus without incurring the penalties for excessive foliage within the exhibit (see Chapter 6).

3 **Llala Palm Tree:** This South American rainforest tree is a favorite of rainforest animals from South America. Note you can fit four llala palms into a single terrain tile.

4 **Acacia Caffra Tree:** This tree is a favorite with animals from the African savannah.

5 **Bamboo:** This is the specific bamboo variety preferred by pandas and is classified as Highlands foliage in *Zoo Tycoon*. It's a must-have when you're building a giant panda exhibit; otherwise, don't bother.

FREEFORM EVOLUTION

When you're playing a scenario, the evolution of your zoo is guided by the scenario's winning conditions. In addition, the full range of *Zoo Tycoon*'s "standard" structures and animals is available right from the start of the scenario. Turning a profit is very easy: All it takes is a couple of well-designed exhibits, a restaurant, an animal theater, and a carousel. This allows you to focus on the scenario goals without worrying about the cash flow, especially since every scenario includes ample starting money.

Things are harder in a freeform game, particularly if you choose the Hard level. When you begin, the availability of animals, foliage, and all types of zoo structures (including fencing!) is extremely limited. New animals, structures, and objects become available on the first day of every third calendar month; fortunately, it's just a two-month wait till the 1st of March and the first set of new choices. Subsequently, new animal species, foliage types, and zoo structures become available in June 1st, September 1st, and December 1st of the first year of the game. The December set is the last; from this point on, new options may only be acquired through relevant research.

The sections that follow describe the choices available to you at the start of the game and at each subsequent milestone. They also include relevant comments and advice. Of course, things are vastly different at the Easy level (where you start with $75,000 in starting money) compared to the Hard level (where you get only $10,000). The advice given here is aimed at players who chose to start with little money.

All listings follow the order set out in the game.

> ## NOTE
>
> *Two new animals are made available when you complete the two very advanced scenarios: "Paradise Island" and "Breeding Giant Pandas." Victory in either scenario unlocks a "mystery beast" that is subsequently available for adoption in all freeform games.*

START: JANUARY 1ST, YEAR ONE

Available animal species: Zebra, Thomson's gazelle, giraffe, lion, moose, grizzly, chimpanzee, Bengal tiger.

Zoo buildings: Soda and candy vending machines, restroom, gift stand, four basic types of animal shelters.

Foliage and rock types: Very, very basic. The umbrella acacia makes good savannah habitats possible; rainforest foliage is represented by only a bush and a fern. There are next to no choices for other habitat types (deciduous forest, coniferous forest, highlands, etc.) and insufficient foliage to successfully re-create any habitat type except the African savannah. The medium rock is the biggest available rock type.

Exhibit fencing: Chain-link and iron bar.

Decorative fencing and zoo scenery objects: Cast iron and post-and-rope decorative fencing; trashcan, bench, wooden picnic table, small fountain. Spiral topiary, hedge, and flowerbed are decorative foliage choices, but don't go spending money on zoo beauty at this stage!

Path types: Dirt, concrete. Concrete's nicer, but much more expensive. Stick to dirt for now.

Comments: This will be the toughest two months of your tenure. The vast majority of your income will come from admission fees; you should focus on creating the best exhibit(s) possible in order to have at least a few zoo benefactors writing out checks at the end of this period. Note that the best moves to make in your first couple of months depend on the type of map you've chosen. The comments that follow assume that you've chosen a relatively uncomplicated, flat map (such as Large Grass Zoo). This is the best, least complicated choice for your first few freeform games of *Zoo Tycoon*.

The foliage choices limit you to building African savannah exhibits. The starting money on the Hard level allows you to build two spacious, high-quality exhibits (as long as you use cheap chain-link fencing). This is because your money will multiply thanks to a $10,000 grant you'll receive when you run out of starting money.

Bulldoze anything that can be sold for money, including existing paths (they're usually worth a pretty penny—see Figure 5.5). Select dirt path to save money and build a big crossroads a few tiles away from the entrance, as recommended throughout this book. Leave space open next to the entrance and lay down a long path across the one leading to the entrance. Then build just two big exhibits, locating them at the ends of that long stretch of path. All zoo guests will want to see both exhibits and will put in quite a lot of mileage walking back and forth.

Locate candy and soda vending machines with accompanying trashcans at the crossroads, build a restroom on either side of the zoo entrance, and put a bench or two along the path to the washroom. Purchasing a gift stand won't increase zoo income, but may help you achieve higher guest happiness (thus increasing your chances of winning over a new benefactor). The best gift stand spot in the early game tends to be at the entrance crossroads, which sees particularly heavy guest traffic.

Concentrate on fine-tuning the exhibits so that your animals hit a high happiness level right away; you want to get them reproducing as quickly as possible. You should get the Silver Plaque for Excellence in Exhibit Design in

TIP

Build your first exhibits between the outer zoo wall and your new path. This will let you use the zoo wall as an exhibit barrier and thus save some money.

your very first month of operation. Unfortunately these come without any cash attached, but it will give you something nice to look at in the Zoo Status/Awards panel.

Don't forget about the expense involved in hiring a zookeeper and a single maintenance worker! The maintenance worker isn't really necessary in the first month; however, you might have problems getting the $300 together over the next couple of months, and then there'll be no one to take care of the trash-cans.

FIGURE 5.5:

Bulldozing the cobblestone path shown here nets over $4,000—an instant 40% increase in starting cash when you play at the Hard level.

Adopting a pair of lions for one exhibit, and pairs of zebras and gazelles for the other, works particularly well. Set admission price at $19 to maximize income. You'll probably want to save money by not doing any research for the first few months!

MARCH 1ST, YEAR ONE

New animal species: Olive baboon, common wildebeest, black bear, Siberian tiger, gray wolf, American bighorn sheep, emperor penguin, saltwater croco-dile.

New zoo buildings: Hot dog stand, drink stand. Don't let the appearance of a giraffe shelter tempt you into adopting this expensive animal—not just yet.

New foliage: The mangrove tree is the most significant addition; it makes Bengal tiger exhibits possible. Aquatic and highland foliage allow you to consider a saltwater crocodile or an American bighorn sheep. The large rock becomes available, greatly simplifying exhibit design.

New exhibit fencing: Stickpole (with and without windows).

New decorative fencing and zoo scenery objects: The white rail decorative fence (which is favored by children); lots of new zoo scenery choices (fountain, exhibit sign, three types of observation areas, statue, lamp, new topiaries and flowerbeds). You still shouldn't be spending any money on zoo beauty.

New path types: Asphalt; it's better than dirt, but you'll be changing in a few months to cobblestone or brick paths anyway.

Comments: Everything's up to the zoo benefactors! If you've succeeded in attracting a few, and they're feeling generous, you may be able to expand your zoo by a couple of exhibits. The saltwater crocodile and the Bengal tiger are the best choices; group them together some distance away from the other exhibits to start your new rainforest theme area. It's probably best to add a long section of path to the one that runs directly toward the zoo entrance. This way, zoo guests will have to walk to all three ends of the zoo to view all the exhibits on display.

Whether you build new exhibits or not, you should purchase a hot dog stand plus the obligatory trashcan, and a couple of picnic tables. The drink stand can wait a while.

Consider adding a few benches in strategic spots if a Guest List survey shows some are low on energy.

You most probably won't have a lot of money to play around with. If you do have a bit extra, see if you can bring one of your exhibits up to 99% suitability. Success will net you the Golden Plaque for Excellence in Exhibit Design, which comes with $15,000 attached—really handy at this stage of the game.

> **TIP**
>
> *Adding a pair of wildebeest to the zebra and gazelle exhibit is a good move; hopefully you've built it big enough! A tiny amount of habitat tweaking may be necessary—wildebeest are slightly more demanding than gazelles and zebras. However, you'll still be able to manage with just one zookeeper if you keep an eye on things yourself, and move him around as necessary.*

June 1st, Year One

New animal species: Black rhinoceros, hippopotamus, leopard, African warthog, American bison, jaguar, polar bear, gemsbok, camel.

New zoo buildings: Ice cream stand, gift shop. The newly available full–sized wood shelter is a solid choice for many exhibits.

New foliage: The plot thickens greatly with the addition of numerous new foliage types. These finally make deciduous and coniferous forest animal species a real option; the habitats in question can be further enhanced with the newly available rock formations. Rainforest, highland, and desert habitats are also now feasible. New decorative foliage additions include a king-size flowerbed (double aesthetics bonus when compared with the standard flowerbed) and a new topiary.

New exhibit fencing: The post-and-rail fence, which is quite sufficient to contain most herbivores.

New decorative fencing and zoo scenery objects: You still shouldn't be spending too much money on zoo scenery items—well, maybe a few sections of decorative fencing here and there; the brick wall becomes available, providing a big aesthetic bonus if you can afford it. The bighorn statue and zoo map are two new decorative choices that will test your resolve not to spend money on anything but the practical brick wall. They're nice!

New path types: Sand path; it ranks on par with the dirt path, beauty-wise.

Comments: Your strategy with regard to exhibits in this period will depend on how much money you have. If you're a little short on cash, your best choice is to adopt animals that are relatively undemanding and don't need companions.

NOTE

Regardless of anything else, you should receive the Blue Ribbon for providing quality animal care at the start of this period.

TIP

Periodically review exhibits for tiles of wrinkled terrain (see Figure 5.6). This indicates that the terrain has been trampled by the animals to the point where it no longer counts toward the suitability of the exhibit. Replace the trampled tiles with new ones; you'll see plenty of happy faces!

Dashing tycoons with a bit of money behind them should consider extending the main zoo entrance path still further, and building a couple of exhibits well away from any others. The extra mileage clocked by your guests will result in sharply increased food/drink profits, but will also necessitate hiring an extra zookeeper (you may also want to hire another maintenance worker). You may find it expedient to build an extra hot dog stand; make a point of purchasing one or even two ice cream stands. A drink stand becomes a profitable proposition at this point; you may want to supplement it with a couple of soda machines and provide strategic backup in the form of an extra restroom at the far, desert end of your zoo. Save up some money for the 1st of September! By now, you should be seeing a steady stream of money coming in from sale of food and drink items.

FIGURE 5.6:

This bit of ground here needs replacing. Monitor exhibits for wear and tear; it's not limited to fencing.

SEPTEMBER 1ST, YEAR ONE

New animal species: Elephant, cheetah, spotted hyena, ostrich, mandrill, ibex, arctic wolf, California sea lion.

New zoo buildings: The good times are here! New buildings include burger and pizza shacks, an elephant ride, and most importantly, an animal theater.

Finally, the family restroom makes its triumphant appearance; immediately replace all existing restrooms with this deluxe model.

New foliage: All habitats receive additional foliage choices. The Himalayan pine is especially noteworthy; it lets you build a quality Siberian tiger exhibit, which usually results in plenty of tiger cubs. New desert foliage lets you refine desert exhibits. Ignore the new flowerbed and topiary models; any beauty expenditures should be concentrated in a different area—see below. Fancy rock formations that become available (stone ruins, waterfall rock formation, highland rock formation) help boost exhibit suitability to new levels.

New exhibit fencing: Concrete, plexiglas, woodslat (with windows and without). Concrete and plexiglas fencing is extremely useful: The first offers privacy, the second is the best type of barrier for containing primates.

New decorative fencing and zoo scenery objects: The picket fence and the duck pond become available. The duck pond is an especially good, guest-happiness-boosting choice for any important rest areas/squares/plazas.

New path types: The cobblestone path becomes available, and you should instantly sell existing dirt paths and replace them with cobblestone for a big, permanent aesthetic boost. Line them with low brick walls where appropriate; don't forget to leave gaps for the zookeepers!

> **TIP**
>
> *Adding a pair of ostriches to the exhibit with gazelles, zebras, and wildebeest lets you easily achieve a prized goal: creating an exhibit containing four different species. This provides zoo guests with an extra happiness boost.*

Comments: The arrival of September 1st tends to be a watershed event thanks to the advent of the animal theater—build one immediately! Build an elephant ride as well, placing it thoughtfully; it's time to consider beginning work on big squares and/or plazas in places where you envisage major intersections.

Your zoo should have four to six exhibits by now. Concentrate your expenditures on zoo infrastructure instead of adopting new animals. You may also want to consider widening main paths to two lanes if you haven't done so already. The money situation should allow you to initiate research, even if only at the lowest level of funding; refer to the sections earlier in this chapter for research advice.

This period is best spent attending to zoo layout and guest amenities. However, if you have been slow in building exhibits, put a priority on having at least four, preferably more.

December 1st, Year One

New animal species: African buffalo, greater flamingo, kangaroo, anteater, markhor.

New zoo buildings: The availability of the restaurant and the carousel ushers in a new era of prosperity. The compost building is also an option as long as you remember to place it far away from everything else (it does not require an access path). Finally, the Japanese garden has big happiness-boosting potential and also scores big points on the aesthetic scale.

New foliage: The most notable addition is the Japanese maple, which is unequaled for landscaping purposes (wild olive and pacific dogwood are two other good choices). All remaining "standard" exhibit foliage becomes available; any new additions will have to be researched. You'll see yet another type of flowerbed and a new topiary. You can finally spend money on such items with a clear conscience!

New exhibit fencing: The rock fence, with windows or not, is the sole—somewhat unexciting—new addition.

New decorative fencing and zoo scenery objects: The low hedge fence is unbeatable for lining exhibit walls, approaches to restrooms, etc.; it can be squeezed in almost anywhere.

New path types: The brick path ranks on par with the cobblestone in aesthetic terms.

Comments: Everything that doesn't require research becomes available at this point. This is a signal to begin research if you haven't done so yet. However, the top priorities are building a restaurant and a carousel; don't hesitate to build two of each if you have the money, but place them wisely. Remember that a restaurant combines food and drink with restroom, trash, and rest facilities. Carousels are great hits with children; all in all you should see a significant increase in guest happiness after investing in these buildings.

At this point, you've completed the initial stage in your zoo's development. You should have half a dozen exhibits, a steady stream of new guests (it's entirely possible to record 200 guests without lowering the admission price), and a steady stream of incoming dollars. You should precede any further expansion by hiring extra maintenance workers and possibly a third zookeeper; this will give you an idea of how much you can spend. If you find yourself short, consider adding a moneymaking building or two instead of an exhibit.

If you're well heeled, and building new exhibits, try to place them some distance away from any existing exhibits. Remember, it doesn't hurt to have empty space in between that can be filled in later; guests will walk more and spend more. The only downside is that you'll have to hire a new zookeeper for the faraway exhibits; however, you'll still come out far ahead in the long run. If in doubt, simply place a restaurant nearby; it will easily pay for *two* new zookeepers.

TIP

Remember that you can put the same species in more than one exhibit if it helps raise exhibit attractiveness. For instance, the African buffalo isn't such a hot item, but the exhibit is fairly cheap, and adding a pair of ostriches will radically increase its attractiveness even if you've already got ostriches in another exhibit.

THE BEST ZOO IN THE WORLD

THE BEST ZOO IN THE WORLD IS A ZOO WITH A **100** RATING. YOUR ZOO'S RATING IS SHOWN BY THE BAR NEXT TO THE ZOO STATUS BUTTON—HOLDING THE MOUSE CURSOR OVER IT WILL BRING UP A TOOLTIP GIVING YOU THE EXACT PERCENTAGE. AS YOU MIGHT EXPECT, YOUR ZOO'S RATING IS A VERY IMPORTANT INDICATOR OF YOUR WORTH AS A ZOO ADMINISTRATOR; IT ALSO DETERMINES HOW MUCH YOU CAN REASONABLY CHARGE FOR ZOO ADMISSION (SEE CHAPTER 7 FOR DETAILS). MOST SCENARIOS MAKE IT A WINNING CONDITION TO ACHIEVE A CERTAIN ZOO RATING; THE NUMBERS VARY FROM **50** TO **80**. THE MAXIMUM ZOO RATING POSSIBLE IS **100**; WHEN YOU START A NEW GAME, THE "STARTING" ZOO RATING IS DETERMINED BY FACTORS SUCH AS GAME MAP AESTHETICS AND STARTING CASH.

NEEDLESS TO SAY, ACHIEVING A ZOO RATING OVER **80** ISN'T EASY. IT IS NOT ENOUGH TO EXCEL IN SELECTED AREAS; YOU MUST EXCEL AT EVERYTHING. THIS IS BECAUSE THE ZOO RATING ITSELF IS THE RESULT OF MANY INDEPENDENT CALCULATIONS, WITH HAPPINESS AMONG YOUR ZOO'S POPULATION (BOTH HUMANS AND ANIMALS) ACCOUNTING FOR NO LESS THAN **50%**. THIS CHAPTER EXAMINES THE FACTORS THAT CONTRIBUTE TO ZOO RATING, AND ENDS WITH A LIST OF GAME PRIZES: AWARDS AND DONATIONS YOU'LL RECEIVE IN RECOGNITION OF YOUR OUTSTANDING WORK.

What Is Zoo Rating?

Zoo rating is determined by seven factors:

- **Animal happiness** accounts for up to 25% of your zoo rating. Maintaining a high level of animal happiness is easy in a small zoo but gets progressively more difficult as your zoo grows. Increasingly big crowds of people may upset the animals, and it's always more difficult to care for 20 exhibits than it is for 2.

- **Animal health** accounts for up to 15% of your zoo rating. Having sick animals will bring you a penalty proportional to the number of animals in your zoo. For example, 1 sick animal out of 10 (10%) will reduce the health bonus to 13.5%, and 5 sick animals out of 10 (50%) will reduce it to 7.5%. As with animal happiness, the fewer animals you have, the easier it is to keep all of them healthy—at least until you research Animal Antibiotics (see Chapter 6).

- **Species diversity** accounts for up to 10% of your zoo rating. The diversity bonus is proportional to the number of species in your zoo. If your zoo exhibits 22 out of the 44 "standard" species in *Zoo Tycoon* (excluding the mystery beasts)—that is, 50%—you'll gain 5% in zoo rating. Naturally, you have to build a very big zoo to get the full 10% bonus for species diversity.

- **Zoo beauty** accounts for up to 10% of your zoo rating. The actual beauty bonus is calculated in a somewhat complex manner, which is fully explained in "The Importance of Looking Good," later on in this chapter. Keeping a big zoo beautiful is difficult because large numbers of guests mean lots of trash, and trash is bad for beauty.

- **Zoo value** can account for up to 10% of your zoo rating. Zoo value is shown at the bottom of the Zoo Status panel and constitutes the sum total of zoo cash and the cash you'd get for selling everything within zoo walls. The way the actual bonus is calculated is fully explained in "The Importance of Being Rich," later on in this chapter. You need a zoo value of $30,000 to get the maximum 10% boost to zoo rating; this means the zoo value boost is maxed out right at the start of many games (all you need is $30,000 in starting cash and zoo structures/objects).

✍ **Zoo research**—the number of research programs completed—accounts for up to 5% of your zoo rating. The contribution research makes to zoo rating is fully explained in "The Importance of Zoo Research," later on in this chapter.

✍ **Guest happiness** can account for up to 25% of your zoo rating. High levels of guest happiness aren't hard to achieve once you've got several well-designed exhibits and a few attractions; however, the many guests you draw this way can easily cause crowded conditions, which leads to a drop in guest happiness.

Now that you know what influences zoo rating, let's look at each factor in detail, starting with the most important: the animals, of course!

THE ANIMAL ANGLE

The animals exhibited in your zoo determine up to 50% of your zoo's rating. Animal happiness is the most important single factor, followed by animal health and species diversity. The following sections examine each of these contributing factors in detail.

ANIMAL HAPPINESS

Animal happiness can be responsible for up to 25% of your zoo's rating. The exact number is arrived at by calculating average animal happiness and multiplying it by 25% (0.25).

For example, say your new zoo contains a total of four animals, with respective happiness levels of 60, 70, 80, and 90. Dividing the sum of these numbers (300) by 4 will yield the average animal happiness level: 75. Seventy-five multiplied by 0.25 gives 18.75; therefore, your zoo's rating will increase by 18.75 percentage points. You can check on average animal happiness by holding the mouse cursor over the bar to the right of the Animal List button.

As you know from preceding chapters, animal happiness is affected by many different factors. Here's a checklist of things to watch:

✍ **Habitat suitability:** As you know from Chapter 3, different animal species have different habitat acceptance levels. Some may require a habitat suitability of only 50% in order to stay happy; others have much more exacting requirements.

🐾 **The presence of other animals:** Many animals require the companionship of other animals of the same species. There's an upper limit to each species' sociability as well; Chapter 3 has the details.

🐾 **Stimulation:** Animal toys and visits from the zookeeper boost animal happiness. There's also such a thing as negative stimulation, and animals that feel crowded by too many zoo guests may become unhappy.

🐾 **Absence of hunger:** A hungry animal will eventually become an angry animal, regardless of species and no matter how perfect everything else happens to be.

Some factors contributing to an animal's happiness level are beyond your control. For instance, all animals dislike captivity to a lesser or greater extent and suffer periodical bouts of sadness. However, the cunning tycoon can offset such negative influences with crafty maneuvers, two examples of which are provided in the section that follows.

A Tip Straight from the Stable

This is the legendary, surefire tip that will let you achieve high levels of animal happiness without cheating—well, without *really* cheating. It comes straight from *Zoo Tycoon*'s designer, Adam Levesque:

"Foliage density is done on a full-tile basis. Meaning, once one foliage object has been placed in a tile (even if that object takes up less than a tile, so that you can put four of those objects in one tile), that tile doesn't count anymore for purposes of having too much foliage. So the player can put more foliage objects (if they take up less than one tile) in a tile with an existing object and get the object bonus—but not the negative hit for having too much foliage.

"Try this out by building an exhibit for the zebras. Make sure any foliage you place takes up less than a tile (an umbrella acacia tree, for example). Keep placing trees in separate tiles until you get an angry face from the zebra. Once that happens, look at the exhibit suitability value. Now, fill up the other 'spaces' in the tiles with those trees. Notice that the zebra will have a smiley face, even though you are technically putting in more foliage than they like."

An example of this in practice is shown in Figure 6.1.

FIGURE 6.1:
Placing multiple trees within a single tile helps keep animal prima donnas content.

HAPPINESS IS BEING WHERE YOU BELONG

If all else fails and you must quickly boost animal happiness because a scenario deadline is just around the corner, try the following:

1 Pause the game.

2 Put all zookeepers into exhibits. You'll most likely have more exhibits than zookeepers, so put them in with the most unhappy animals first. Place the zookeepers as far away from the exhibit gate as you can; it may be advisable to imprison them permanently by blocking the exit (by moving the exhibit gate behind a rock, animal shelter, etc., which costs nothing). If you're rich, consider hiring more zookeepers specifically for the purpose of imprisoning one in each exhibit.

3 Restart the game. Keep an eye on the zookeepers, dropping them back into exhibits as appropriate. Their presence will keep animal happiness high, particularly if you've also researched at least one level of zookeeper training.

ANIMAL HEALTH

Animal health is linked to animal happiness, inasmuch as a happy animal is less likely to fall sick. When all the animals in your zoo are healthy, your zoo's rating receives a 15 percentage-point bonus. The presence of sick animals reduces this bonus proportionately: If half the animals in your zoo are sick, you'll receive 7.5. Naturally, if half the animals in your zoo are sick, you're facing a catastrophe, and zoo rating bonuses are a side issue. In practice, you can expect to steadily receive the full 15% as long as you build highly suitable exhibits and keep them clean. Acquiring a panda may throw some sand into the works: These sickly animals demand constant care from dedicated zookeepers.

> ## NOTE
>
> *Remember to keep the exhibits free of poo. Each pile of poo reduces habitat suitability in proportion to the habitat size: small exhibits can suffer a 1% decrease in suitability for every pile of poo. Review the total number of animals in an exhibit every time a new one is born, and don't hesitate to hire an extra zookeeper worker to keep things under control.*

SPECIES DIVERSITY

This is, somewhat surprisingly, the least important of the animal-related factors that influence zoo rating. It can boost your zoo's rating by up to 10 percentage points, with the actual bonus being determined by the percentage of available species that is represented in your zoo. There are 44 animal species in *Zoo Tycoon* (not counting the "mystery" beasts, which aren't used in this calculation). If your zoo exhibits 22 species (50%), then you'll receive half of the species diversity bonus, which amounts to a 5 percentage-point boost in zoo rating.

As you can see, *Zoo Tycoon* places the emphasis on quality before quantity. You should always strive to make the animals you have as happy as possible before acquiring new ones. Some scenarios may force small deviations from this rule; indeed, one or two allow you to cheat by adopting new species at the last moment—right before the end of the scenario—and placing them in makeshift exhibits. This way, the newly acquired animals don't have time to get seriously unhappy before the bell rings, and you can happily meet the number of exhibited species needed to win. Note that this maneuver won't always work; it lowers average habitat suitability, which often appears as yet another winning condition. See Chapter 8 for further details.

RATING LOOKS, MONEY, AND SMARTS

Zoo rating is also significantly influenced by zoo aesthetics, finances, and research. These three factors can jointly account for up to 25% of your rating total; the following sections examine each in turn.

Note that aesthetics, finances, and research are areas of activity over which you have absolute control. However, maximizing the rating bonus available from these three sources isn't easy: Progress in the aesthetic and research departments costs money, which weakens zoo finances.

THE IMPORTANCE OF LOOKING GOOD

Having a beautiful zoo can boost your zoo rating by up to 10%. Calculating your zoo's aesthetic value is a complex process, as there are four types of guests with different aesthetic preferences: what's beautiful to a boy may look outright nasty to an adult woman. The game adds up the aesthetic value of all the objects on the zoo map (even those outside the zoo walls) separately for each guest type (man, woman, boy, girl), and then divides the resulting sum by 4 to yield average guest aesthetic value. The average guest aesthetic value is subsequently divided by the number of all zoo tiles that feature anything—be it a rock, a tree, part of exhibit fencing, or a section of path. The resulting number is the zoo beauty percentage boost to zoo rating; it's capped at 10, or 10%.

The small size of the bonus to zoo rating may lead you to assume that aesthetics aren't that important, and that all the items listed in Appendix C play a minimal role. However, remember that zoo aesthetics play a significant role in guest happiness (see Chapter 4), which means that they influence zoo rating both directly and indirectly. Now you know why *Zoo Tycoon* has so many zoo scenery choices!

WHAT'S NICE, WHAT'S NOT

The numerous zoo structures, foliage types, and zoo objects that have an aesthetic impact are listed in Appendix C. Items not listed there are neutral in aesthetic terms. If you don't feel like wading through a sea of numbers, here are the main points:

- There is no uglier thing than trash, and trashcans—overflowing or not—come in a close second. So place trashcans only where they are really needed: in the vicinity of food/drink vending machines, stands, and shacks. Extra trashcans in areas where people merely consume food and drink are an option, not always a necessity. Naturally, your numerous and vigilant maintenance workers should be swooping down on every piece of trash the moment it hits the ground.

- Take a long look at your zoo before spending money on beautifying items. Upgrading a dirt path to cobblestone may have a greater impact than purchasing 20 fountains, statues, and topiaries. Be aware of the aesthetic impact of such mundane items as exhibit fencing, path types, and guest amenities.

- Make all rest areas beautiful. Guests linger in rest areas—that's the point of a rest area, after all. This offers you an opportunity to bombard them with beauty for a prolonged period of time.

  - Erase the negative impact of trashcans and basic restrooms by placing pleasant-looking items nearby. Guests using the basic bog will feel they're undergoing a near-mystical experience if you flank the entrance with topiaries, line the approach with hedges, and perhaps even put a lamp behind the building for those who get lost. The rude presence of a couple of trashcans can be balanced by a nearby flowerbed.

  - Choose the right decorative item for each spot. Use decorative fencing along the paths; lining a path on both sides is a particularly good move. In addition to providing an aesthetic boost, decorative fencing is a good tool for regulating traffic. It ensures that guests don't stray from the path and can also be used to mark off a rest area within a wider expanse. Note that some items (like low hedges or a lamp) can be squeezed in almost anywhere.

As a general rule, decorative objects that cost more are more effective: A fountain that costs $800 has greater aesthetic value than a $500 fountain. You should always place such costly additions where they can be viewed by the most people (see Figure 6.2):

- **Zoo entrance:** This is an area through which every guest must pass at least twice.

- **Path intersections:** Don't neglect intersections, including those where you chose not to build a square or a plaza.

TIP

Lining a brick or cobblestone path with low brick walls is the best path/decorative fence combination in terms of aesthetic value.

- **Approaches to attractions:** For instance, a couple of elephant topiaries at the entrance to an elephant ride will make squeamish adults feel better about the approaching experience.

- **Approaches to restrooms:** These get particularly heavy traffic in big zoos, no matter how many restrooms you build.

- **Rest areas:** As previously mentioned, it's an easy way to boost happiness because you can mercilessly inflict beauty on resting guests.

FIGURE 6.2:
A rest area should always contain plenty of beautiful sights.

Remember that while beauty is important, spending money on flowerbeds and fountains has a relatively low priority. Always run a check on animal happiness and zoo traffic flow before committing yourself to sizable investments in zoo beauty! Unhappy animals and crowded guests will erase any gains decorative items provide.

THE IMPORTANCE OF BEING RICH

Zoo value can boost your zoo rating by up to 10 percentage points. When this bonus is calculated, the cash you have on hand and the value (sale price) of everything within zoo walls is counted and divided by 300. The resulting number is then expressed as a percentage and divided by 10. To cut to the chase: To get the maximum 10 percentage point bonus to zoo rating, zoo value

must equal or exceed $30,000. If you have less, the rating bonus will be smaller (for instance, $15,000 will yield a 5% bonus). This seldom happens in practice, and is limited to freeform games played on high-difficulty level. Even then, zoo value is likely to climb past $30,000 within the space of the first few months.

THE IMPORTANCE OF ZOO RESEARCH

Zoo research can improve your zoo's rating by up to 5 percentage points. The exact boost to zoo rating from this source depends on the number of research programs completed.

NOTE

Chapter 5 discusses zoo research programs in detail.

You must complete all the research possible in the game to obtain the full 5 percentage points. If you haven't, the number of completed programs is divided by the number of all the programs to yield a fraction. This fraction is then multiplied by 5% (0.05) to calculate the zoo rating boost from this particular source.

Although the final result may seem insignificant, the research bonus can be of great value when you're trying to win a scenario that features a high zoo rating as one of the winning conditions.

RATING GUEST HAPPINESS

Up to 25% of your zoo rating is determined by the happiness of guests in your zoo. The happiness value used in this calculation is average guest happiness: the total of all the individual happiness levels divided by the number of guests. You can check average guest happiness at any time by examining the bar to the right of the Guest List button (see Figure 6.3).

Average guest happiness is expressed as a percentage and divided by 4 to calculate the actual boost to zoo rating. Consequently an average guest happiness of 50% will result in a 12.5% increase in zoo rating while an average happiness of 80% nets you a 20% increase, and so on.

You probably know quite a lot about guest happiness from Chapter 4, but here's a summary of the main points:

🐾 Make sure all your guests' needs are met: Use the Guest List to examine the circumstances of needy guests. Remember to check on crowd density before building anything; many guest frustrations are caused by crowded conditions, not the lack of appropriate amenities in your zoo.

🐾 Give your guests continuous happiness boosts by exhibiting only happy, healthy animals in well-designed and thoughtfully arranged habitats.

Check the zoo rating, average animal happiness, and average guest happiness bars periodically, keeping all three green at all times.

✋ Group exhibits into theme areas, and make sure you have an exhibit containing at least four different animal species (savannah animals are perfect for this purpose).

✋ Provide numerous attractions. Do not be afraid to build several attractions of a given kind (4 animal theaters, 5 Japanese gardens, 6 petting zoos, 286 carousels, etc.)

✋ Keep prices low. Chapter 7 is full of wisdom on the subject of turning a profit; you'll find it's possible to cut prices across the board and still make a pile. Even the most efficient tycoon will occasionally be forced to raise the admission price in order to reduce crowding; however, prices charged inside the zoo should always be kept on the low side.

✋ Keep the zoo beautiful. You'll find it very easy if you just follow the basic rules explained earlier on in this chapter. Appendices B and C contain data that will let you purchase and place new structures with pinpoint precision.

NOTE

The petting zoo and the Japanese garden are the best all-around choices for making both adults and children happy. Unfortunately, neither structure makes money, and both can contain only four zoo guests at a time.

ZOO AWARDS AND DONATIONS

Zoo awards and donations are tokens of recognition of your worth as a tycoon; they do not influence your zoo rating. Zoo donations consist of big monetary grants. Zoo awards come in two varieties—with cash attached, and without. In both cases, your newly won award will be displayed on the Zoo Status panel (Awards tab; see Figure 6.4). Both awards and donations are one-time affairs; you cannot receive the same one twice.

The following sections examine all the awards and donations that you can win in *Zoo Tycoon*. Each entry is followed by comments on how you get it and the role it plays in the game.

FIGURE 6.4:

It's always nice to have a few tokens of recognition of your genius.

AWARDS

Each listing below contains the following award info:

- **Award name and class:** Most awards come in two colors, so to speak: silver and gold. You may also collect a couple of handsome blue ribbons.

- **Condition:** This describes what you must do to receive the award.

- **Benefit (if applicable):** Some awards come with a big chunk of cash.

Comments: These briefly discuss how difficult it is to win the award, what winning it says about you, and the usefulness of the money attached.

EXCELLENCE IN EXHIBIT DESIGN—SILVER PLAQUE

Condition: You must create an exhibit with a suitability rating of at least 90%.

Comments: This award is almost automatic in all *Zoo Tycoon* games, except for the very early scenarios. You'll get it with your first exhibit when playing a freeform game, because you know very well that *Zoo Tycoon* puts quality before quantity, and that a single excellent exhibit is better than three shoddy ones.

EXCELLENCE IN EXHIBIT DESIGN—GOLD PLAQUE

Condition: You must create an exhibit with a suitability rating of at least 99%.

Benefit: $15,000

Comments: Every alert tycoon will recognize this award as a great opportunity to pocket some serious cash. It's not expensive to turn an acceptable exhibit into a great exhibit; it just takes some patience. The expense is tiny compared with the prize, so you should make a point of snagging this award with your very first exhibit in all freeform games (it makes playing at the Hard level much easier). It's also within easy reach in almost all scenarios and instantly provides you with funds for zoo expansion.

MOST POPULAR ZOO—SILVER CERTIFICATE

Condition: You must record 500 guests in your zoo.

Comments: Tycoons who are aware of the inherent difficulties of people management will recognize this symbolic award as a sign of true achievement. Scoring this certificate means that you have reached professional tycoon status, but you may miss receiving one in early game scenarios because of their small scale. The same applies to freeform games played on small maps.

MOST POPULAR ZOO—GOLD CERTIFICATE

Condition: You must record 1,000 guests in your zoo.

Benefit: $25,000

Comments: Receiving this award means that you're a master at playing *Zoo Tycoon*. Building a zoo capable of happily handling 1,000 guests simultaneously is only possible in advanced scenarios and medium- to big-map freeform games. Unfortunately, the money that comes with the reward usually doesn't mean that much: You'll be rolling in dough by the time you clock 1,000 guests, if only because a large percentage of them will be buying something at any given time.

BEST ZOO—SILVER TROPHY

Condition: Your zoo rating must reach 90.

Comments: This award means your zoo is nearing perfection. It is quite difficult to achieve the required zoo rating, and receiving the Silver Trophy means you're a very talented tycoon. No cash attached, but it's pretty nice to look at in the Awards panel.

BEST ZOO—GOLD TROPHY

Condition: Your zoo rating must reach 95.

Benefit: $25,000

Comments: This award is very hard to get. It may involve both substantial expenditures on refinements to your zoo and underhanded maneuvers such as setting the admission price to $100 to reduce numbers of guests in your zoo. Getting the Gold Trophy means you're the consummate tycoon, and the money attached is loose change for someone of your abilities. You definitely won't collect this award without building a big zoo in which numerous animal species and zoo guests are all glowing with happiness.

HIGHEST CUSTOMER SATISFACTION—BLUE RIBBON

Condition: Average guest happiness must reach 95.

Benefit: $25,000

Comments: This is a very useful award that's relatively easy to get in the middle stages of zoo development. In most scenario and freeform games, this award follows the building of chosen zoo attractions and animal houses. If it proves elusive, try temporarily reducing the number of guests in your zoo by hiking the admission price and simultaneously slashing prices inside the zoo to increase the happiness of the guests you do have. The money you receive can be very handy in the early-middle game.

QUALITY ANIMAL CARE—BLUE RIBBON

Condition: Animal happiness must reach 98, and six game months must have passed.

Benefit: $5,000

Comments: This particular ribbon is won automatically by every efficient tycoon in every freeform game and all but the earliest scenarios. It is relatively easy to achieve this level of happiness among your animals once their habitats have been made comfortable. Getting an extra five grand six months into the game is very convenient because at this stage, it's frequently the equivalent of a couple months' income.

DIVERSE SPECIES—SILVER PLAQUE

Condition: At least 10 different animal species must be represented in your zoo.

Comments: As you can guess from the circumstances under which this award is handed out, you'll get it automatically in all but the earliest scenarios and all but purposely stunted freeform games. It doesn't really mean that much, but it looks good.

DIVERSE SPECIES—GOLD PLAQUE

Condition: At least 30 different animal species must be represented in your zoo.

Benefit: $30,000

Comments: This award is a possibility only in very advanced scenarios and big freeform games. Smaller scenarios allow it only in theory: You'll be too busy meeting winning conditions to worry about acquiring additional animal species. Running a zoo with 30 different species involves a lot of skill, and receiving this award means you're a gold-plated tycoon of high caliber. Unfortunately, a tycoon of this caliber considers 30 grand small change.

HIGHEST QUALITY EXHIBITS—SILVER CERTIFICATE

Condition: Your zoo must have 10 or more exhibits with suitability ratings of 80 or better.

Comments: You should receive this certificate upon building your tenth exhibit, as tweaking a habitat to 80% suitability is not that difficult. This certificate marks an early milestone in zoo development and confirms that you're on the road to tycoonhood. It's the basic tycoon diploma.

HIGHEST QUALITY EXHIBITS—GOLD CERTIFICATE

Condition: Your zoo must have 25 or more exhibits with a suitability rating of 85 or better.

Benefit: $40,000

Comments: You'll receive this certificate upon building your 25th exhibit. It marks another, bigger milestone in zoo development and comes with a nice wad of cash. Unfortunately, when playing a scenario, you'll be too busy with scenario winning conditions to set your sights on this award (meeting a scenario's winning condition won't necessarily get it for you). It's much easier to get in big freeform games, but any prize money received in the later stages of a freeform game counts for little. This award is an advanced tycoon diploma that indicates you're both capable and hardworking. By the time you get it, you'll have many other awards.

DONATIONS

There are three kinds of donations in Zoo Tycoon; all are examined in detail in Chapter 7. Here, we'll discuss just one kind: the donations that you receive as a result of a specific event. These happen only once per game and are of two types:

- An emergency grant of $10,000, which you receive the first time your cash drops below $1,000. This donation makes playing freeform games at the Hard level (when your starting cash equals 10 grand as well) much easier because it allows you to immediately build a second exhibit.

🖐 Donations received when an endangered species reproduces in your zoo. All endangered species have to be researched first, and most are fairly demanding (see Chapter 3 for details). The amount you receive is $10,000 in all cases but one: If you can get the sickly, shy, pathologically inhibited pandas to reproduce, you'll be rewarded with $50,000. Researching endangered species was fully discussed in Chapter 5; just to remind you, the endangered species include the lowland gorilla, white Bengal tiger, black leopard, snow leopard, okapi, and finally the giant panda (they're most often researched in that order).

Building the best zoo in the world is expensive. The successful tycoon must be very skillful at making money—and this is precisely what the next chapter is about.

RUNNING A SUCCESSFUL ZOO REQUIRES COMPETENT MONEY MANAGEMENT. IT'S NOT ENOUGH TO MAKE SURE YOUR ZOO EARNS ENOUGH MONEY TO COVER RUNNING EXPENSES SUCH AS EMPLOYEE WAGES AND EXHIBIT UPKEEP COSTS. YOU'LL ALSO NEED TO ACCUMULATE SUBSTANTIAL SUMS IN ORDER TO AFFORD NEW ANIMALS, EXHIBITS, ZOO BUILDINGS, EMPLOYEES, AND SO ON. THIS IN TURN NECESSITATES BIG MONTHLY PROFITS, ESPECIALLY WHEN YOU'RE PLAYING AN ADVANCED SCENARIO (THE EARLY SCENARIOS FEATURE PLENTY OF STARTING MONEY, WHICH ALLOWS YOU TO COAST TO VICTORY).

YOU'LL FIND THAT MAKING MONEY IN ZOO TYCOON IS NOT VERY DIFFICULT. WHAT IS DIFFICULT, WHEN YOU'RE PLAYING A SCENARIO GAME, IS MAKING ENOUGH MONEY IN TIME TO MEET ALL THE WINNING CONDITIONS. ALTHOUGH THESE NEVER INCLUDE ACHIEVING A SPECIFIC ZOO VALUE, YOU'LL FIND THAT WINNING AN ADVANCED SCENARIO REQUIRES A LOT OF HEAVY SPENDING. AND THIS IS WHERE THIS CHAPTER SHOULD BE HELPFUL—IT TAKES A CLOSE LOOK AT MONEY IN ZOO TYCOON, EXAMINING ZOO INCOME, EXPENDITURES, AND PROFIT.

UNDERSTANDING ZOO FINANCES

When playing the game, you obtain financial information from five sources:

🐾 **The available cash display at the bottom of the game screen:** This shows you how much you've got in the till at any given moment. Beware—it can be misleading, particularly near the end of the month when fixed monthly expenses are about to kick in.

🐾 **The Zoo Status/Information panel (top tab):** This panel shows and lets you adjust the admission price; it also lists the number of current zoo benefactors, which is useful for making financial forecasts. More benefactors mean more money on the first of each month. Since they contribute a random amount between $100 and $300, you may have distinctly lucky and unlucky months in that respect. New benefactors can appear on any day; if any existing benefactors resign, they do so on the first day of the month. Note that the bottom of the panel contains listings for zoo funds and zoo value.

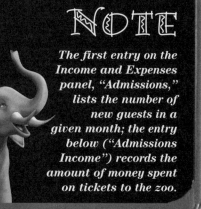

NOTE

The first entry on the Income and Expenses panel, "Admissions," lists the number of new guests in a given month; the entry below ("Admissions Income") records the amount of money spent on tickets to the zoo.

🐾 **The Zoo Status/Income and Expenses panel (second tab from top):** This lists all of the zoo's monthly income and expenses, covering four consecutive months. It lets you examine existing trends as well as the effects of your cunning financial moves. It's updated daily and is the most important single source of financial info in the game.

🐾 **The Zoo Status/Graphs panel (third tab from top):** This panel lists zoo rating, donations, profit, and attendance over a 12-month period. It's also updated daily. You can choose between graph and bar charts by clicking on the appropriate button.

🐾 **The Building Information panel (see Figure 7.1):** Clicking the icons in this panel will let you see a building's total income and upkeep costs as well as average monthly figures. It's updated every time a purchase is made.

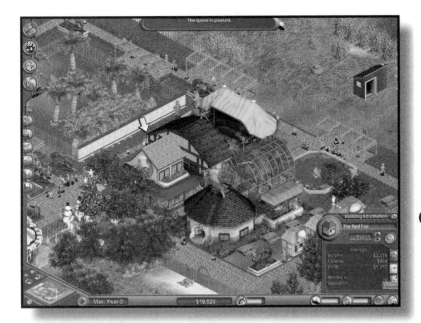

The Building Information panel lets you determine a building's profitability.

The Zoo Income and Expenses panel lists no less than four separate sources of income along with six types of expenditures. The sections that follow examine each in detail.

ZOO INCOME

The Income and Expenses panel lists four sources of income; however, two of those cover a variety of profits. Each source of income is discussed in the following sections. Note that the order here follows the order in which they appear on the Income and Expenses panel; this does not reflect their relative importance.

ADMISSIONS INCOME

Admissions income is your zoo's most important source of income in its first year of operation. It continues to be an important contributor to zoo coffers throughout the game, but its importance slips when the profits from concessions really start kicking in and monthly donations grow four figures (see Figure 7.2).

FIGURE 7.2:

The importance of admissions income tends to drop as time goes by.

You'll quickly be made aware of a certain discrepancy between the number of new guests and the money you bring in through zoo admissions. This is because the nice guys at developer Blue Fang took mercy on all the ambitious but green tycoons and instructed each zoo guest to buy three adult and one child's ticket. When you set the admission price to $10, each guest will spend $35 on admission; when you set it to $20, you'll collect $70 per guest, and so on. When you raise admission prices above $30, you'll see little girls spending $100 at a time, which should rightly teach you to treat all children with respect and sympathy and cater to all their needs (numerous ice cream stands, carousels, etc.).

Admission price falls into one of six categories: free ($0), very cheap ($0.25–$9), cheap ($9.25–$19), normal ($19.25–$29), expensive ($29.25–$49), and very expensive ($49.25 and more). As explained in Chapter 4, admission price is important in determining how frequently guests show up at the front gate; a lower price *category* means more guests. It makes little difference whether you set the price to $19 or $12, since both are in the "cheap" category; it makes a meaningful difference when you set it at $20 instead of $19 or $30 instead of $29, because that moves you up into the next category. Remember to set your admission price at the top end of the current category at all times!

Here's a quick rundown on the price categories:

- **Free admission ($0):** Letting people in for free is an emergency measure when you very quickly need lots of new guests in your zoo. Otherwise, set admission to free only when you're feeling insanely generous, and remain aware that a huge influx of new guests may lead to a drop in average guest happiness.

- **Very cheap admission ($0.25–$9):** This works exceptionally well when you want to get plenty of new guests fast while still collecting a few dollars along the way. In terms of attracting guests, there's little difference between free and very cheap admission once your zoo has reached a rating of 60 or more, which is easily achieved even by very green tycoons.

- **Cheap admission ($9.25–$19):** If your zoo rating is in the higher seventies or better, you'll see the message "Guests are saying that the entrance fee is really good value." This admission price gets you a large number of new guests every month; it works well from the start in most scenarios and all freeform games.

- **Normal admission ($19.25–$29):** This becomes a good choice once your zoo rating exceeds 80. You'll still be getting reasonably large numbers of new guests while making thousands of dollars from admission fees alone. Overall, normal price is the most profitable setting of them all.

- **Expensive admission ($29.25–$49):** You'll make your zoo expensive to restrict the number of new guests. Whether you set the dollar figure at $30 or $49, you'll still see a small but fairly constant number of new guests showing up every month if your zoo rating is high enough (over 80).

> ## NOTE
>
> *The number of paying guests is also influenced by your zoo rating: A higher rating means guests are willing to pay more. Push your zoo rating into the eighties as quickly as possible; this allows you to charge at the top end of the "normal" admission category and still get many new zoo guests every month. Remember that marketing can increase zoo rating for guest creation purposes.*

🖐 **Very expensive admission ($49.25–$100):** In an emergency, this setting will quickly reduce the number of guests in your zoo, thus boosting average guest happiness. Of course, you might as well go whole hog and set it to $100. If your zoo is excellent, occasional guests will still show up, which might result in unexpectedly high admission fees. You probably won't feel happy about that, since this price setting is used specifically to discourage new guests.

INCOME FROM PRIVATE DONATIONS

This listing on the Zoo Status/Income and Expenses panel includes money from four similar sources:

🖐 **The small change dropped into appropriate boxes in the zoo:** As you play, you'll see the dollar figure representing private donations grow on a day-to-day basis, going up a few bucks per day. This is caused by all those coins and small bills stuffed into donation boxes outside zoo exhibits. Clicking an exhibit gate and selecting the Donations icon in the Exhibit Information panel will tell you how much money has been put into the invisible donation box outside that particular exhibit.

🖐 **The big checks written out on the first day of each month by registered zoo benefactors:** These checks will account for most of your income from donations; you should court benefactors assiduously by creating excellent exhibits and improving your zoo rating in every feasible way. Note that a new benefactor may only be created upon the exit of a guest from your zoo; there's a wait involved. Each benefactor may contribute anything between $100 and $300 at a time; once your zoo has attracted over 20 benefactors, life is nice.

🖐 **The checks that come with top zoo awards.** As a rule, a silver award of any type (plaque, trophy, certificate, etc.) comes without money attached, while a golden award comes with a nice big check (up to $40,000). The award money can help you achieve a particular goal if the timing's right, but you shouldn't really count on award income until you get good at the game.

🖐 **Awards for endangered species reproduction:** Upon getting an endangered species (any of the species that have to be researched) to reproduce in your zoo, you'll receive a donation. Usually it's $10,000, but a baby panda is worth $50,000. This donation is only awarded once for every endangered species, so it hardly constitutes steady income; all the same, it can be a lifesaver in later scenarios.

Overall, donations can constitute up to 30% of zoo income if you make sure guest happiness stays in the nineties. In many games, the donated dollars amount to between 15% and 20% of monthly income. Ideally, they should cover all zoo staff expenses.

MONEYMAKING CONCESSIONS

Zoo concessions are your the most important, colorful, and entertaining source of income. As mentioned in Chapter 2, concessions include four types that sell food or drink (vending machines, stands, shacks, and restaurants), gift stands and gift shops, and finally three types of attractions: carousels, animal theaters, and elephant rides. Note that other types of attractions may not make money but remain important for the purposes of making guests happy; some also have high aesthetic value (see Figure 7.3).

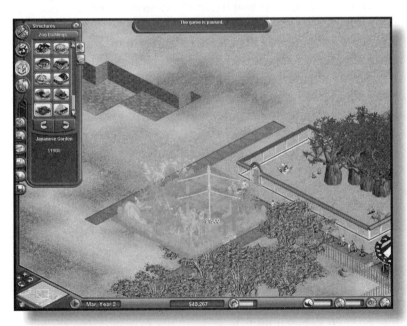

FIGURE 7.3:

A profitless Japanese garden is still a valuable addition to your zoo.

The prices charged in your zoo have an effect on guest happiness. There are three price thresholds:

Cheap: 50% of the item's default price

Normal: 100% of the default item price

Expensive: 150% of the item's default price

You *can* give away items for free if you really want to, but that won't boost guest happiness any more than selling them cheaply.

The dollar figure you'll see next to the Concessions listing on the Zoo Status/Income and Expenses panel can be misleading; it represents gross profit from all your moneymaking structures—concession upkeep costs are accounted for in Zoo Upkeep. The net earning potential of the various types of concessions differs greatly, ranging from the $40 a month earned by a busy vending machine to the $2,000 a month earned by a busy restaurant. Upkeep costs vary from $10 to $500 a month and stay fixed regardless of the number of sales made.

INCOME FROM FOOD AND DRINK CONCESSIONS

In *Zoo Tycoon*, every zoo guest purchases more than one item at a time (two cans of soda, three hot dogs, etc.—examining the Building Info panel while a guest makes a purchase will give you the details). For instance, if you leave the default price of a hot dog at $2, every paying guest will fork over $6.

There are eight types of concessions that sell food or drink, and they are listed in the following bulleted list. Note that the profits quoted apply to concessions selling items at the default price in fairly busy zoos. Profits will vary widely depending on guest numbers, guest happiness, and the amount of time spent by guests in the zoo.

- **Vending machines** cost $50 to build and sell candy or soda. Upkeep costs are $10 per month per machine. Income after upkeep is negligible, topping out at around $50 per month for very busy candy machines. Soda vending machines generally earn less, even given the slightly higher default item price ($1.25 against $1.00 for candy).

- **Ice cream stands** cost only $125 and are good moneymakers, often turning a nicer profit ($250 plus per month) than drink stands. They provide a nice happiness boost to zoo guests as well, and rarely fail to make money; upkeep is $50 a month.

- **Hot dog stands** cost $175 to build. They can make you a pretty penny: They turn a tidy profit *and* stimulate drink sales sharply. Profits at very busy hot dog stands average $300 monthly. Of course, proper location is very important. Upkeep costs $50 a month.

- **Drink stands** cost $250 and have very good earning potential. In freeform games, if you build them as soon as they're available they may barely manage to break even; generally, it makes sense to build them around the time you'll also be building a burger shack. Profits may reach $300 a month, but often are lower—$200 per month after the $50 upkeep cost is quite decent.

- **Burger shacks** cost $250 and are great little moneymakers. They spread happiness among adult zoo guests and tycoons alike, easily averaging $400 and often hitting $500 a month in profit (after the $50 in monthly upkeep costs). They are considerably more efficient at feeding people than the cheaper food stands, but they necessitate extra seating and trashcans for the guests.

- **Pizza shacks** cost $325, but usually make slightly less money than burger joints (upkeep costs are identical at $50 a month). Their big advantage is even greater efficiency; however, this necessitates ample seating and may cause trash problems. They aren't the hottest catering choice in the zoo hospitality business.

- **Restaurants** cost $2,200 to build and $500 per month to run. However, restaurant profits make such considerations totally unimportant; they may approach $3,000 per month (after upkeep). Restaurants include restrooms, seating, and trash disposal, therefore satisfying absolutely all conceivable personal needs of zoo visitors. You should build them wherever they won't be actually losing money (in practice, you must try hard to have a restaurant lose money); the impressive array of guest services is worth it.

INCOME FROM ENTERTAINMENT CONCESSIONS

Moneymaking entertainment concessions consist of three buildings: the animal theater, the carousel, and the elephant ride. The first two are great moneymakers, the third one…lousy. It makes children happy, though. Note that all the money numbers quoted below refer to concessions charging default prices in busy zoos.

- **Animal theaters** tend to edge out carousels as the top money spinners because of lower upkeep costs ($50 a month). They make both adults and children happier, and adults also like the way they look. $700 a month net is a good profit.

- **Carousels** are a hit with everyone, but particularly so with children. Their relatively small size will allow you to squeeze them into vacant areas throughout the zoo; a carousel almost can't fail to make a tidy profit even though it costs $100 in monthly upkeep. On the average, carousels earn just a little bit less than animal theaters (around $650 a month); extremely popular carousels will earn slightly more ($750).

☞ **Elephant rides** should be built only in order to increase guest happiness. They take up more space than carousels and offer meager profits; netting $200 after the $50 monthly upkeep is quite heroic.

INCOME FROM GIFTS STANDS AND GIFT SHOPS

A guest who wants to buy a zoo souvenir but is unable to do so loses happiness. This gives retail gift outlets special significance, and the gift shop can also be a great moneymaker. As usual, the dollar numbers quoted below apply to default price item sales in busy zoos.

☞ **Gift stands** should be treated as a basic guest amenity. Their upkeep costs are quite steep at $50 per month, and it's a busy gift stand that clears $50 in monthly profits. However, you should sprinkle them in strategic spots throughout your zoo and retain most of them in a supporting role even when you've got a couple of busy gift shops. Besides, it's fun to watch the gift seller dive into the stand trunk for the panda, and the cash register sound effect is like a bugle call to anyone with tycoon instincts.

☞ **Gift shops** have to be placed just right in very busy locations: the $200 monthly upkeep cost is painful. The items they sell (zoo coloring books, plastic animal models, stuffed pandas, zoo T-shirts, and so on) may bring higher profits than an animal theater or a carousel. Gift shop roofs feature a joyful koala with a clutch of balloons; it spins round and round when a sale is made, which is very appropriate.

RECYCLING BENEFIT

Recycling income is derived from two sources. The first is the sale of bulldozed zoo stuff: foliage that's already there when you start the game, zoo buildings that have outlived their usefulness, superfluous zoo animals, and the like. The second source of recycling benefit dollars is the compost building, which turns every pile of poo into $50 the moment it's raked up by the zookeeper. This can amount to quite a bit of loot in a large zoo with many animals, and easily hits three figures even in a mid-size zoo.

The compost building that magically turns poo into gold is expensive to build ($1,500), but carries no upkeep cost. Its presence carries a significant aesthetic hit, however, and it definitely requires a sanitary cordon of sorts: Keep guests at least five tiles away, building decorative barriers if necessary. You don't want them to smell the shimmering perfume of the compost heap (see Figure 7.4).

Freeform games give you the freedom to punish undisciplined maintenance workers.

ZOO EXPENSES

There are two kinds of zoo expenses: one-time costs incurred while building something or adopting new animals (construction cost and animal purchase cost), and the ongoing costs of running the zoo (zoo upkeep expenses, employee wages, and optional research and marketing expenses). Both scenarios and freeform games stress making your zoo grow as quickly as possible, so construction costs tend to constitute the greatest single expense, though they may be very high in some months and low in others. Employee wages are usually the second-biggest expense, followed (sometimes closely) by zoo upkeep.

The picture changes sharply if you decide to finance research at the maximum rate. Research costs can total just over $4,000 a month, with marketing throwing in another $1,000 at the maximum funding level. Note that in scenario games, research often isn't voluntary: You must complete certain programs in order to win, and complete them quickly. Marketing is an option if you need to quickly increase the number of guests in your zoo, and can be used in conjunction with a dramatic admission-price slash. However, note that if admission is free, marketing has no extra effect except in zoos with extremely low rating.

TIP

Income from bulldozed zoo stuff plays a very important role at the start of many scenarios and freeform games, giving you extra cash when it's most needed.

The sections that follow look at that various types of zoo expenses. Note that the order here follows the order in which they appear in the game's Zoo Status/Income and Expenses panel.

CONSTRUCTION COSTS

This will be your single biggest expense in all games of *Zoo Tycoon*; quite a lot of the game is spent waiting for that extra few hundred bucks in order to complete building something. You'll find yourself incurring construction costs month after month even if you aren't engaged in expanding your zoo; there's trampled terrain in exhibits to be replaced, and also the phenomenon known as impulse spending ("Oooo, I can fit a duck pond in there").

ANIMAL PURCHASE COSTS

These may briefly become significant in the opening months of a game, but as a rule are dwarfed by construction expenses. Once your zoo has a few exhibits, animal purchase costs quickly fall behind employee wages and zoo upkeep expenses. Their significance is magnified in the more difficult scenarios, where every dollar counts. In freeform games, animal purchase costs are important only in the first few months, quickly becoming of little significance thereafter; they're always dwarfed by the expense of building an exhibit.

ZOO UPKEEP COSTS

Zoo upkeep tends to make the third-biggest hole in the zoo budget. It is a collective term for all the expenses incurred while running the zoo with the exception of employee wages. Thus, it includes the upkeep costs of all the zoo concessions, attractions (advanced exhibits in animal houses!), and animal food.

Zoo upkeep quickly climbs into three figures once you've built a basic zoo (several exhibits, an animal theater, a carousel, a restaurant, and a couple of other concessions). Upkeep costs continue growing as your zoo expands, usually totaling 60% to 70% of the sum spent on employee wages.

EMPLOYEE WAGES

This is the biggest fixed expense that you *must* meet every month, mainly because of the high salaries commanded by the zookeepers—make sure they're really earning their money. The employee wages budget shoots sky-high when you decide to hire tour guides; it can easily wipe out all admission and donation income. Remember that employee wages are promptly deducted from the zoo till on the first day of every month and are also incurred whenever you hire anyone; try to hire as early in the month as you can.

RESEARCH COSTS

Research expenses frequently become a great worry in scenario games, where the need to complete a program quickly competes with the need to build, build, build. The dilemma is whether to start research early at minimum funding (just $26 a day for concurrent Conservation and Research programs) or to invest in moneymaking structures and conduct later research at normal or maximum rates. An all-out research effort costs over four grand a month, which means it may temporarily become the number one expense in some scenario games.

ZOO MARKETING

Zoo marketing is a strictly voluntary option; it definitely pays for itself if your admission price is normal or higher (see "Admissions Income," earlier in this chapter). You'll have little need to resort to zoo marketing in freeform games; as mentioned earlier, it may be useful in scenarios where you need to record a high number of guests in your zoo. You cannot spend more than $1,033 a month on marketing.

THE WAY OF THE TYCOON

Making money in *Zoo Tycoon* isn't difficult. Making money *fast* is. All scenarios—particularly the advanced ones—have a time element that stresses the need to get rich quick, and naturally you'll also be eager to get ahead when playing a freeform game. With this in mind, a few pointers follow to get you underway.

TIP

The mushrooming cost of employee wages can easily be contained if you make a pact with yourself to build a money-making structure every time you hire anyone. A carousel usually pays the wages of a couple of maintenance men, while a restaurant can easily support two zookeepers.

WARNING

Postpone research until you're sure your budget can handle the burden. Putting money-making investments first allows increased research funding later on; while if you strangle early zoo growth through research expenses, you could lose a scenario before you're even halfway through.

149

At the start, concentrate on enticing as many people into your zoo as possible. Set admission prices at cheap or very cheap; free admission doesn't make a big difference compared to cheap, and you might as well make a few bucks on the tickets. Initially, the only new concessions available in a freeform game are vending machines. Set up a couple to cater to guests who enter the zoo already hungry and thirsty, but don't count on making any meaningful money out of them (see Figure 7.5).

FIGURE 7.5:
Most days, the profit from a vending machine wouldn't buy you a burger in your own zoo.

In game scenarios, you'll be able to build animal theaters and carousels right away, and you should grab this opportunity with both hands. A single gift stand for guests who cannot live without a stuffed panda is recommended for both freeform and scenario games.

THE BIG PUSH

Once you have a decent number of people in your zoo (near 100), set up food and drink concessions in earnest. In freeform games, you'll be limited to a hot dog stand and a drink stand; build just the hot dog stand to start with, and follow with the drinks only if you see several guests who are thirsty despite the presence of your excellent soda vending machine. If you're playing a scenario, splurge on a restaurant; try to place it so as to gain maximum turnover.

Examine your zoo to see whether a second animal theater and/or carousel might not be a good idea—building a second carousel is almost invariably a good move! Do not build extra food stands unless you see guests going hungry in spite of the restaurant. When you do begin building extra food concessions, choose ice cream stands and burger shacks over everything else. Limit drink stands to the busiest spots; put soda vending machines elsewhere. You'll need to pause at this point and save some money in order to build a couple of new exhibits. Don't fritter money away on zoo scenery!

TIP

A restaurant has every kind of food available in a zoo.

THE MONEY MACHINE

At this point, your zoo will already have become an efficient money machine, making several thousand in net profit every month. Don't squander this money, especially if you're playing an advanced scenario; establish clear goals and limit spending on anything else. This is a good time to begin research, allocating minimum funding to begin with. When guest numbers approach 300, find a good spot for a second restaurant and place a gift shop on the busiest corner in your zoo; usually that's near the entrance. If the situation's right for a second restaurant, it's also right for a third carousel! They often work well together, and it's about time you started planning things in terms of rest and recreation plazas. As explained in Chapter 2, these work best when sited at the major intersections in your zoo.

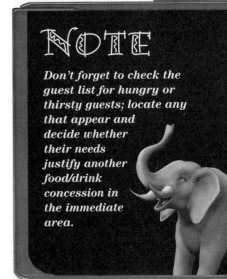

NOTE

Don't forget to check the guest list for hungry or thirsty guests; locate any that appear and decide whether their needs justify another food/drink concession in the immediate area.

Monitor your zookeepers; if you see them clearing up numerous piles of animal dirt, invest in a compost building. Don't buy it earlier; $1,500 is a hefty price tag that's unjustified if you'll be making just a couple hundred dollars a month.

You should be making over $5,000 a month in net profit at this stage. In a scenario, further zoo development will be defined by the requirements of the scenario; in freeform games, you're basically free to do what you please. Given your existing zoo infrastructure, you'll be able to bounce back even from very bad and costly mistakes!

ZOO GAMES

ZOO TYCOON FEATURES THREE TUTORIALS AND 13 SCENARIOS (GAMES THAT ARE WON BY ACHIEVING SET CONDITIONS WITHIN A STRICT TIME LIMIT). YOU MAY ALSO ELECT TO PLAY WHAT IS CALLED A "FREEFORM" GAME ON ONE OF THE 28 MAPS DESIGNED FOR THAT PURPOSE. FREEFORM GAMES HAVE NO TIME LIMIT AND NO DEFINED WINNING CONDITIONS; THEY CONSIST OF BUILDING A ZOO GIVEN A CERTAIN AMOUNT OF STARTING MONEY (LESS MONEY MEANS A HIGHER LEVEL OF DIFFICULTY). IT'S WORTH NOTING THAT EVERY SET SCENARIO CAN BE TURNED INTO A FREEFORM GAME: YOU ALWAYS HAVE THE CHOICE OF CONTINUING TO PLAY AFTER THE WINNING CONDITIONS HAVE BEEN MET. NATURALLY, EVERY COMPLETED SCENARIO MAY BE REPLAYED AS MANY TIMES AS YOU LIKE.

THIS CHAPTER DISCUSSES ZOO TYCOON'S SCENARIOS (WISDOM RELATING TO FREEFORM GAMES IS DISPENSED IN CHAPTER 5). PLAYERS WHO CHOOSE TO COMPLETE ALL THE SET SCENARIOS BEFORE ATTEMPTING A FREEFORM GAME WILL HAVE A NICER FREEFORM EXPERIENCE: WINNING THE LAST TWO SCENARIOS UNLOCKS TWO MYSTERY ANIMALS THAT SUBSEQUENTLY BECOME AVAILABLE IN ALL GAMES.

Zoo Scenarios

The sections that follow contain walkthroughs of each of the game's 13 scenarios. These scenarios are split up into four groups by difficulty level: Beginner, Intermediate, Advanced, and Very Advanced. You must complete all the scenarios in a group to move up in difficulty, but you can play the scenarios within a group in any order you choose. For example, you may begin by playing "Forest Zoo" instead of "Small Zoo" even though it's the third on the list both in the game and here.

Beginner Scenarios

This group contains three scenarios whose aim is to teach you, gradually, to build a functioning zoo with acceptable levels of guest and animal happiness. By the time you play the last scenario in this group you should be a skilled exhibit designer and have a firm grasp of the basic principles of zoo layout.

Small Zoo

Starting money: $75,000

Winning conditions: Achieve a suitability of 60 or more for each of the zoo's 6 exhibits; achieve average animal happiness of 80.

Time: 6 months

Comments: This extremely easy scenario features three ready-made exhibits. After you've put each of the three available animals (giraffe, moose, and camel) into the appropriate exhibit, six new animal species appear on the Adopt Animal menu. You should select three species (lion, kangaroo, and tiger are good choices) and build exhibits for each. The zoo features paths marking the proposed new exhibit sites; the two big square sites are fine, the L-shaped site near the zoo entrance is not (it's quite cramped). Money is absolutely not a problem in this scenario, so give yourself a bit of an extra challenge and select a new site for the third exhibit—it can adjoin the one next to the giraffe exhibit. You will thus have a pair of new exhibits next to the giraffe exhibit.

Create appropriate habitats, referring to the in-game Zookeeper Recommendations and/or Chapter 3 in this book for guidance; you'll easily hit 70+ exhibit suitability. You might have to hire a second zookeeper and a second maintenance worker; assign the zookeepers to three habitats each. Your average animal happiness should be somewhere in the 90s; wait for six months, and that's it. Ambitious tycoons should use that time to tinker with the exhibits, noting how small changes affect exhibit suitability. You should also consider setting up a gift stand or two; the Littleburg Zoo already has a burger shack, a drink stand, and a family restroom—no further investments are necessary in these areas.

Seasideville Zoo

Starting money: $70,000

Winning conditions: Achieve a suitability rating of 60 or more for 5 exhibits, an average animal happiness of 80 or better, and an average guest happiness of 80 or more.

Time: 6 months

Comments: This scenario is very similar to "Small Zoo": the winning conditions are almost identical, except that that you have to do a lot more with slightly less money, building six exhibits instead of three. A guest happiness of 80 or more is practically a given without any extra effort on your part.

This scenario features a fully laid out zoo; all you have to do is build the exhibits. It's not worth your while to bulldoze everything and start from scratch; the only adjustments you might want to make are in the area behind the gift stand (see Figure 8.1). Note that an area near the zoo entrance contains a large patch of savannah grass, and that desert habitats will automatically be cheaper given the large expanses of sand. The starting money is just enough to build six good exhibits; you'll also get a $10,000 donation if you get into financial trouble. Keep in mind that you

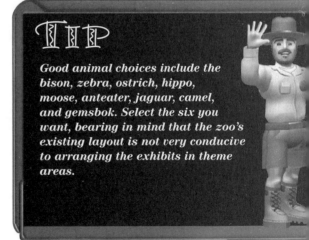

> **TIP**
>
> *Good animal choices include the bison, zebra, ostrich, hippo, moose, anteater, jaguar, camel, and gemsbok. Select the six you want, bearing in mind that the zoo's existing layout is not very conducive to arranging the exhibits in theme areas.*

have to hire two zookeepers and at least one maintenance worker! You have 12 animal species to choose from; winning conditions do not reward mixing two or more species in the same exhibit.

If you're building with the game running, keep an eye on the clock; there are only six months in which to complete the scenario. Consider buying an animal theater and a carousel even though you don't really need the income; it's what a tycoon would do.

Guests are saying the entrance fee is a really good value.

Jun, Year 1 $19,330   Animal Happiness %

FIGURE 8.1:

Tweaking the existing zoo layout lets you build exhibits at minimum cost.

Forest Zoo

Starting money: $50,000

Winning conditions: Achieve a suitability rating of 70 or more for 6 exhibits, an average animal happiness of 85 or better, and a zoo rating of 60 or more. You cannot adopt any animals in this scenario; 6 species are provided in 2 sets of 3.

Time: 12 months

Comments: This scenario introduces you to the importance of zoo rating. Reaching the rating of 60 isn't difficult—the zoos in the two previous scenarios easily top 70. The difficulty lies in the fact that you're required to design and build a zoo all by yourself. The existing layout—a central red brick parking lot with three picnic tables and two vending machines—does not work well. Bulldozing everything (including the assorted trees, rocks, and bushes in the area within zoo walls) will yield over $7,400 in extra cash. Given the $10,000 emergency grant, you'll have just enough to build a very nice zoo complete with all the guest amenities, numerous attractions, and six good exhibits.

After bulldozing the entire zoo area, lay out a big crossroads five or six tiles away from the zoo entrance. Extend the paths parallel to the zoo wall so that you can fit several exhibits in between. Remember to allow for two tiles of space between the exhibit fence and the path; this will let you easily mark out observation areas (see Figure 8.2). You'll have to build a total of six exhibits, as a second series of three species quickly follows the first three animals you're told to house at the start. You begin the scenario with a Bengal tiger, a grizzly bear, and a black rhino; the next three species consist of two zebras, a saltwater crocodile, and a clouded leopard.

You might want to arrange the rainforest animals (tiger, leopard, and crocodile) on one side of the gate, and put the rhino and zebras (both African savannah species) on the other. The grizzly exhibit can be put next to the path leading straight to the entrance. Don't extend this path beyond the stream embankment!

WARNING

Don't get taken in and attempt to utilize existing terrain features when building exhibits. The stream that flows through the center of the zoo area contains a mixture of fresh and salt water, and its embankment makes building anything awkward. It's better to satisfy the grizzly's preference for hilly terrain by raising the center of its exhibit a few levels.

FIGURE 8.2:
Use the zoo walls to save money when building exhibits. Note the observation areas on both sides of the path.

Build exhibits while making sure there's plenty of empty space left near the big crossroads. When you're finished with the first three exhibits, unpause the game briefly to receive the second set of animals. Build exhibits for those right

away, unpausing the game only to get the $10,000 emergency money. Then finish the job by placing guest amenities and attractions in the vicinity of the crossroads. Make sure you include a couple of family washrooms right away! Having met all scenario objectives, pass the time by improving exhibits, adding beautifying touches, and observing what goes on.

INTERMEDIATE SCENARIOS

There are four intermediate scenarios in the game; by the time you've completed them, you'll be a highly skilled tycoon. The first two scenarios— "Revitalize Burkitsville Zoo" and "Inner City Zoo"—emphasize economy and building exhibits containing more than one species; "Inner City Zoo" also stresses the importance of good zoo design. Winning the third scenario— "Saving the Great Cats"—requires deft financial management, completing certain research, and building many high-quality exhibits. Finally, "Endangered Species Zoo" will test your newly acquired tycoon abilities: You'll have to research a series of endangered species and subsequently get them to *reproduce.* Yes, the jokes are over.

REVITALIZE BURKITSVILLE ZOO

Starting money: $30,000

Winning conditions: Exhibit a total of 8 species in the zoo; achieve an average animal happiness of 75 or better and a zoo rating of 50 or more.

Time: 12 months

Comments: This scenario challenges your tycoon abilities by putting you in control of a zoo built by a moron in a hurry. The animals are suffocating in tiny cage-like exhibits whose walls are a hodgepodge of different types of fencing. They're quite unhappy about it, and the only thing that makes sense is to sell all the animals and bulldoze every existing structure in the zoo (including the lonely burger shack). This move will yield over $14,500; given the automatic $10,000 emergency grant that kicks in when your starting cash runs out, you'll have a total of nearly $55,000 at your disposal.

Inspired tycoons should begin by laying out the standard big crossroads half a dozen tiles from the zoo entrance, then building a big African savannah exhibit—big enough to contain a dozen animals belonging to four different species (zebra, gazelle, wildebeest, and ostrich). Make sure zoo guests walk all around it by placing a big attraction on the other end: a hippo/flamingo exhibit and a lion exhibit work equally well (see Figure 8.3). If you choose lions, you'll most likely have enough cash to add one more savannah exhibit, for a total of six different species.

Use your remaining money on money-making attractions and food/drink concessions. Place them strategically: food stands plus a restroom near the entrance and a restaurant at the far end work well. Add an animal theater and a carousel and you're all set to begin raking in serious cash—you'll be making over $5,000 a month by the end of the first quarter. Set admission to $19 or less in the first couple of months to attract many new zoo guests. Remember to hire an extra zookeeper; one will not be able to handle all the animals.

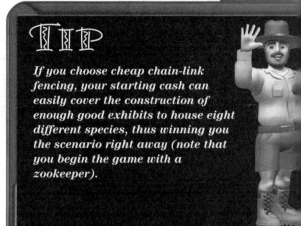

If you choose cheap chain-link fencing, your starting cash can easily cover the construction of enough good exhibits to house eight different species, thus winning you the scenario right away (note that you begin the game with a zookeeper).

By the time September comes along, you'll have enough money to build an exhibit (or exhibits) for two more species. Consider the hippo/flamingo combination if you haven't built it yet; it's very popular with the zoo guests. Also, make a little bit of extra effort and you can easily win both the Silver Plaque for Excellence in Exhibit Design and the Blue Ribbon for Quality Animal Care; this second award comes with $5,000 attached.

FIGURE 8.3:

The new Burkitsville zoo, on the cusp of adding the scenario-winning exhibit. All these exhibits and structures can be built for under $55,000.

INNER CITY ZOO

Starting money: $25,000

Winning conditions: Exhibit a total of 6 species in the zoo; achieve an average animal happiness of 78 or better, an average guest happiness of 85 or better, and a zoo rating of 55 or more.

Time: 12 months

Comments: Time to test your zoo design skills! In this scenario, you take over a tiny L-shaped zoo bisected by a path that makes it look even smaller. The existing path suggests building a series of tiny exhibits; don't do that! Bulldoze the path (worth $400+), then spend some money leveling the small mounds, dips, and hillocks that break up the zoo area here and there. Leave the big slope at the base of the L untouched; you'll win without building anything there, and anyway it's half-ready for a highlands species habitat.

Your sharp tycoon sense will have told you that the way to win this scenario is to build a big mixed exhibit. Lay out a new path, running it right next to the zoo wall. Then lay out a big African savannah exhibit using the other zoo wall for a back fence. If you use chain-link fencing, the extra $10,000 you'll get upon running out of starting cash will enable you to build exhibits for two more species right away. However, you can also win with true style and class by concentrating on building a high-quality mixed savannah exhibit (four species), then adding a couple of moneymaking attractions (animal theater, carousel). Build a couple of cheap food/drink concessions, one attraction, and a restroom near the zoo entrance; put the other attraction and a restaurant at the other end (see Figure 8.4).

You might be tempted to wait awhile with the restaurant because of the high upkeep cost; if so, keep an eye on your cash as February approaches. Expenses that kick in on the first of the month can make building a restaurant impossible; it's better to swallow a small initial loss and build it right at the start of the scenario.

Set the admission price to just below $19, and within a couple of months you'll be making good money. You should be able to build one or two exhibits for two more species by June or July; kangaroo and saltwater crocodile are two economical choices that are quite attractive to the paying public. Otherwise, build more savannah exhibits, turning your whole zoo into a savannah theme area. You should be able complete this scenario with just one zookeeper.

You'll quickly see that the main difficulty in winning this scenario is keeping guest happiness over 85. As your zoo fills up, tempers will fray!

Concentrate on making money and adding touches that increase guest happiness (stone or brick paths, decorative fencing, a couple of gift stands, a petting zoo, a duck pond, etc.). If you've got the money, consider researching Animal Houses at full throttle ($66 a day). Hike the admission price sharply a couple of months before the end of the scenario; you'll see average guest happiness increase as guest numbers dwindle. Keep an eye on happiness levels as the scenario deadline approaches!

If you don't build anything that necessitates a trashcan, you can economize by not hiring a mainte- nance worker for the first couple of months!

FIGURE 8.4:

The Inner City Zoo nine months into the scenario— note the zoo layout empha- sizing good traffic flow.

Saving the Great Cats

Starting money: $30,000

Winning conditions: Adopt 2 lions, 2 leopards, 2 cheetahs, 2 Siberian tigers, 2 Bengal tigers, 2 white Bengal tigers, 2 jaguars, 2 clouded leopards, 2 black leop- ards, and 2 snow leopards; achieve a suitability of 85 or more for all cat exhibits and an average animal happiness of 90 or better.

Time: 18 months

Comments: This is the first really challenging scenario. You'll have to research Endangered Animals in order to adopt white Bengal tigers, black leopards, and snow leopards (don't waste time and money researching the panda). You'd do well to also research Animal Shelters until you get the snowy rock cave and all the animal toys (the leopards' favorite, the cat climbing tree, comes last). Some quick counting will tell you that you need to build 10 exhibits, most of which will be fairly expensive, and ultimately hire at least three and preferably four or five zookeepers. Of course, the starting money isn't enough to achieve a quarter of the scenario objectives; you'll have to build a thriving, rich zoo, and build it fast.

Begin by bulldozing everything inside the zoo walls; you'll collect nearly $11,000 in extra starting cash. Build the standard entrance crossways and extend the path on the flat side of the zoo entrance. It's a good idea to build a series of exhibits along the zoo wall, thus saving some money on fencing. It's best simply to build one very long exhibit between the path and the zoo wall, then divide it into two. Note that the cats you're to adopt fall into distinct groups: three from the African savannah, five from rain-forest jungles around the world, one from the hilly coniferous forests of Siberia, and one from the Tibetan highlands.

It makes sense to start by building exhibits for the savannah animals. You'll need plenty of space for the cheetah exhibit; plan things accordingly (see Figure 8.5). The African leopard also requires a lot of room. One of the difficulties of this scenario is making enough money to build big and well-appointed exhibits that easily keep the animals happy. You should consider using chain-link fencing; tycoons who opt for luxury concrete walls and iron bars will have to flip a financial somersault or two to complete this scenario.

Once you've got three species of cats settled in, build an animal theater and at least a couple of carousels right away. You have to start making money fast in this scenario! Set the admission price to cheap ($19) and get things rolling. Start researching Animal Shelters and Endangered Animals at the minimum funding level right away; this will enable you to pull off a little financial coup later in the game. Concentrate on adding a restaurant as soon as the second month begins and fine-tuning the existing exhibits before building new ones. Put rock caves into your exhibits as soon as the relevant research is completed; this is the favorite shelter of all the cats required by this scenario with the exception of the snow leopard. You should aim at pushing exhibit suitability well past 85 if possible, or an untimely pile of poo could lose you the scenario!

Continue to build new exhibits along the zoo wall; use existing terrain features for the Siberian tiger and the snow leopard—it's not a bad idea to leave these two till the very end. Build rain-forest exhibits first; by the time you've gotten a Bengal tiger, a jaguar, and a clouded leopard you'll have completed the scenario's required Endangered Animals programs. Discontinue Conservation research, concentrating on completing Animal Enrichment (toys) and subsequently Animal Care.

Don't hesitate to spend money on a second restaurant and other profitable concessions. It's possible to quickly record 500 guests in this scenario—you don't have to worry about guest happiness and thus you don't have to worry about crowding. Make sure you have enough money to fine-tune each exhibit with the adopted animals already inside; you don't want them to get unhappy. The snow leopard is very demanding in this respect, and its exhibit involves raising the elevation of the hills already present in the zoo. If you find yourself short of money, grit your teeth till just before the end of the penultimate month of the scenario, then sell attractions and concessions built earlier to avoid paying upkeep costs on the first of the last month.

TIP

After you've researched Animal Fertility, your white Bengal tigers and black leopards will likely reward you by reproducing; this will net you a total of $20,000. In addition, all the other cats (with the possible exception of the cheetahs) will be multiplying on a regular basis. You'll make quite a few bucks from animal sales in this scenario, which is just as well.

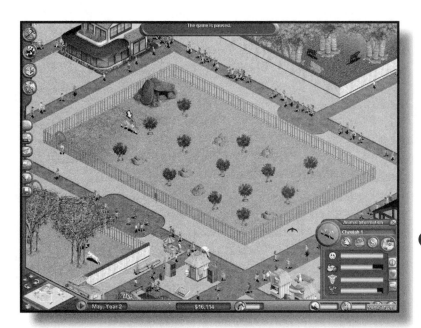

FIGURE 8.5:

The moody cheetah requires a big, expensive exhibit.

ENDANGERED SPECIES ZOO

Starting money: $50,000

Winning conditions: Achieve a suitability rating of 70 or better for 12 or more exhibits, an average animal happiness of 90 or more, a zoo rating of at least 70, and an average guest happiness of 93 or more; get white Bengal tigers, black leopards, and okapis to reproduce in your zoo.

Time: 18 months

Comments: This scenario tends to be easier than "Saving the Great Cats." You begin the game with an almost complete, ready-made small zoo (the two exhibits need work). You should sell the animals and bulldoze everything, except perhaps the animal theater. You'll get around $40,000 in return, thanks to the numerous trees within the zoo walls.

Given the first emergency financial donation, you'll have $100,000 in starting cash at your disposal, and that makes this scenario a bit of a walkover. $100,000 in starting cash means it's relatively easy to build 12 excellent exhibits and get the three endangered species to do their stuff (appropriate research is needed first). The only real problem lies in achieving the high average guest happiness required to win. Twelve exhibits and a commensurate number of attractions will beget many new zoo guests, and toward the end of the scenario you may have to institute drastic hikes in admission price in order to cut the number of guests in your zoo.

Once you're done with bulldozing, two courses of action suggest themselves. One is to proceed in the traditional manner, building three or so very good exhibits and adding extra attractions and concessions as time goes on, while conducting the mandatory research (Endangered Species, Animal Care, and Animal Shelters). It is easy to win the scenario in this manner. Note that you do not actually have to *possess* the baby animals when the scenario ends. All that counts is getting the three endangered species to reproduce; you may safely sell the offspring—of course you should wait till they turn into adults.

Dashing tycoons might want to try a more original approach (see Figure 8.6). After bulldozing everything, except maybe the animal theater, don't build anything; set research to maximum funding instead, choosing Endangered Species (Conservation) and Animal Shelters (the rock cave is the preferred shelter of both leopards and tigers). You'll notice that in this

> **NOTE**
>
> *Animal happiness of 90 is almost a given for any tycoon who has managed to get this far in the scenarios; so is an exhibit suitability of 70 or more (in fact, this scenario offers a good opportunity to win the Gold Plaque for Excellence in Exhibit Design).*

scenario, endangered species are researched in a different order: You begin with the white Bengal tiger. Given maximum funding, it takes only seven days to complete the white Bengal program, and you can immediately build an exhibit for this species. This will begin attracting zoo guests, so you should also build paths and a couple of additional attractions (such as the carousel). The rock cave becomes available after 10 days; switch Research funding from Animal Shelters to Animal Care.

TIP

Stop researching Endangered Species once you have the okapi; concentrate on Animal Care. Completion of the Animal Fertility program is usually followed by the birth of a baby to one of your endangered species pairs (usually white Bengals are the first to reproduce), which gets you a check for $10,000.

If you continue funding research at the maximum level, the black leopard becomes available for adoption in February and the okapi at the beginning of March. By mid-March, you should have all three endangered species represented by happy pairs of animals in high-quality (90+ suitability) exhibits.

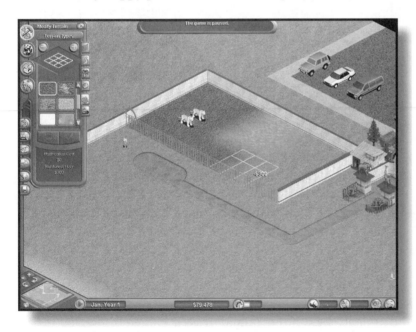

FIGURE 8.6:
Consider delaying construction until the first endangered species becomes available.

Continue expanding your zoo in the traditional manner from this point on. You'll have plenty of money and little trouble with building nine more exhibits; consider adopting rainforest species to add to the three you've already got. If your white tigers, black leopards, and okapis are slow to reproduce, consider adopting extra pairs of these species. The exhibits you build for them count toward victory, and you'll immediately double the chances for successful reproduction.

ADVANCED SCENARIOS

The four scenarios in this group will test your tycoon abilities in a variety of ways. "Island Zoo" emphasizes zoo and exhibit design; "African Savannah Zoo" focuses on your moneymaking skills; "Mountain Zoo" requires you to design and build a big zoo in very difficult terrain; and finally, "Tropical Rainforest Zoo" is a long, tough test of your zoo management skills. You'll find that achieving high ratings in all areas— animal and guest happiness, zoo rating, and exhibit suitability—is one thing; maintaining those ratings is another.

ISLAND ZOO

Starting money: $40,000

Winning conditions: Achieve a suitability rating of 85 or more for 10 exhibits; a zoo rating of 75 or better; an average animal happiness of 93 or better; and an average guest happiness of 93 or more.

Time: 24 months

Comments: There's little room for mistakes in this scenario; you must build a 10-exhibit zoo on a series of small to medium-size islands linked by narrow causeways. There's only one way to leave enough room for exhibits of reasonable size, and that's to make all paths hug the shore. The same applies when building exhibit fencing; you must grab every tile of available terrain, and you're sure to come up with some interesting exhibit shapes! You can get up to around $6,000 by bulldozing paths and decorative fencing in the far half of the zoo area; yes, it's possible to fit in 10 exhibits and several attractions and concessions in slightly less than half of the available space.

The secret lies in choosing animal species that don't mind solitary existence and have reasonable personal space requirements. Many cats belong to this category—consult Chapter 3 of this book for relevant data on individual animal species. Of course it's best if the animal of your choice is also highly attractive to zoo guests, but don't let that make you ignore the advantages of unexciting but undemanding animals such as the anteater.

You'll notice that the guests in this scenario are easy to please as long as you keep their numbers down (see Figure 8.7). Since this scenario requires you to make a lot of money (only one emergency donation of $10,000 is available), you must build an animal theater and a carousel right away. It's a good idea to utilize the area right behind the zoo gate for the big theater and a restaurant; this way you'll make sure a lot of people visit the theater on the way in and even more hit the restaurant on the way out. Consider building a second restaurant later on and forgetting about any stands or shacks; this will let you get by without a maintenance man for the first year. You'll have to hire one later to repair the fencing.

FIGURE 8.7:

High guest and animal happiness are both needed to win this scenario. Note the umbrella acacia forests in the savannah exhibits.

The zoo layout forced on you in this scenario necessitates your hiring a zookeeper for every two exhibits. You'll have to be very vigilant about any piles of poo that appear on the scene—given the small size of the exhibits, a single pile can drop the suitability rating by 1%. If you don't pay attention, you might lose the scenario simply because a zookeeper was daydreaming in the final week! Naturally, you should do what you can to boost exhibit suitability far above 85 (you should collect the Golden Plaque for Excellence in Exhibit Design). Given very high exhibit suitability and frequent zookeeper visits, achieving average animal happiness in the high 90s won't be a problem!

African Savannah Zoo

Starting money: $20,000

Winning conditions: Exhibit 20 or more animals from the African savannah while achieving a suitability rating of 80 or more for 13 exhibits, a zoo rating of 75 or better, an average animal happiness of 93 or better, and an average guest happiness of 93 or more.

Time: 24 months

Comments: You begin this scenario without much cash; what you do have is a variety of animals imprisoned within six impractical exhibits. If you sell all the animals and bulldoze everything within the zoo walls, you'll receive an extra $47,000. Thrifty tycoons should consider retaining the animals and immediately building new exhibits for all of them with the game paused.

TIP

A compost building is a particularly good investment in this scenario.

The bulldozing immediately removes the greatest obstacle to victory in this scenario, which is low in starting cash; if you include the $10,000 emergency grant, you'll have a total of around $67,000 to start building your zoo. Of course, it's not enough for 13 good exhibits—even though most of the default terrain is savannah grass, which saves a pile. But 67 grand is more than enough to build an efficient money machine producing a steady, rapid stream of cash. Note that you do not have to fit in all the exhibits on the zoo gate side of the river flowing through the zoo grounds. You can always build a bridge to the other side (see Figure 8.8). It also pays to remember that this scenario can be won without conducting any research whatsoever.

You'll have to begin by raising the ravines so that there's a large, flat area next to the zoo entrance. Then proceed to build the zoo following standard procedure: a big junction near the entrance, a line of exhibits along the zoo wall, and so on. Don't forget to build an animal theater and a carousel right at the start and a restaurant a month later. Add extra attractions in various parts of your zoo as time goes on; one attraction/concession for every new exhibit is a good ratio.

You'll have noticed that the winning conditions include having 20 *animals* from the African savannah, not animal species, and that they don't reward putting multiple species into one exhibit. You should set up a couple of mixed exhibits anyway—at the very least the classic hippo/flamingo and gazelle/zebra/wildebeest/ostrich combinations. You might run into difficulty meeting the exhibit suitability requirement for the exhibit with four species; if so, simply build new exhibits for the least happy species (wildebeest and gazelles) and place them there right before the scenario ends. All this maneuvering might be necessary in order to maintain a high level of guest happiness (guests get extra kicks out of mixed exhibits), which is a winning condition; this might also require you to hike admission prices in order to cut down on the crowds in your zoo.

FIGURE 8.8:

Building a bridge across the river is easier when you use a big palette.

Mountain Zoo

Starting money: $50,000

Winning conditions: Exhibit 15 or more animal species in exhibits with a suitability rating of at least 80; achieve a zoo rating of 70 or better and an average animal happiness of at least 90.

Time: 24 months

Comments: This scenario is about making lots of money—fast. You'll notice immediately that the winning conditions reward high-quality exhibits with multiple species (which naturally makes achieving high suitability more difficult). A quick look at the Adoption menu will tell you that building exhibits for every highland or hill-loving species in the game won't be enough. That means

serious dollars will have to be spent on terrain adjustments. Fortunately, bull-dozing everything except for the bit of triple-lane path right by the zoo gate will reward you with around $26,000.

You cannot afford to level an area big enough to contain 15 species. What you must do is create three or more flat areas, taking advantage of existing terrain features as much as possible. Guest happiness is not a concern here, so these exhibit areas can be relatively far away from each other.

Begin by enlarging the flat area right next to the zoo gate. You should have enough space for three exhibits; decide in advance which type of species you want to feature. Animals from the African savannah recommend themselves very strongly because they offer the best opportunities for mixed exhibits. It isn't difficult to bring an exhibit containing four mixed savannah species to a suitability rating of 80; you can even push it a little higher than that. Of course, as the scenario's end approaches, you'll have to be vigilant about replacing trampled terrain tiles and cleaning up poo.

As mentioned earlier, this scenario is about making money fast: You'll need an animal theater, two restaurants, and two carousels at the very least. Do not build all of these right away; wait a month before building the first restaurant and the second carousel, adding a second restaurant a few more months down the road.

Begin the game with your admission price set to cheap, hiking it to normal when you've got over 100 guests in the zoo. Concentrate on creating a complete miniature zoo in the area by the entrance (see Figure 8.9); once you've got a nice little money machine in place, begin expanding. Use a medium to big palette to adjust terrain; it makes sculpting straight, sloped edges easier.

Build paths to neighboring flat areas, which should be big enough to fit in two or three exhibits apiece. It's possible to fit 10 savannah species in the area by the zoo entrance; or play it safe by using the lessons you learned in "Island Zoo," selecting species with small personal-space requirements.

Winning this scenario doesn't require you to complete any research. If you refrain from spending a single dollar on research, you'll meet all the winning conditions several months before the scenario deadline. Use any extra money to hire more zookeepers; this minimizes the threat of a sudden drop in animal happiness or exhibit suitability.

FIGURE 8.9:

This little zoo is making $10,000 a month in profit— thanks to its 28 benefactors.

TROPICAL RAINFOREST ZOO

Starting money: $50,000

Winning conditions: Exhibit 17 or more animal species in exhibits with a suitability rating of at least 90; achieve a zoo rating of 80 or better, an average animal happiness of at least 90, and an average guest happiness of 90 or better.

Time: 36 months

Comments: You won't get away with building a smaller number of mixed species exhibits in this scenario; the high suitability rating required for each exhibit makes it out of the question. But the biggest problem in this scenario isn't finding the money to build 17 exhibits and a set of accompanying conveniences and attractions; it's maintaining high levels of guest happiness after your zoo has grown to a certain size.

You begin with a nice big concrete crossway that works well; don't touch it apart from straightening out the paths. This may necessitate building a bridge to the side of the zoo gate; work with a single-tile palette, raising a row of tiles a couple of levels. Bulldozing everything apart from the existing crossway will net you around $64,000. You can certainly afford to start things with a big bang, and it's likely you won't need any emergency money grants.

This scenario calls for careful planning; you'll be building multiple entertainment and convenience areas in your attempt to make zoo guests really happy. Begin by laying out the first of these near the front gate. Consider adopting a series of rainforest species first, as this will decrease exhibit construction cost; the zoo features rainforest terrain and grass. You have enough starting cash to expand beyond the river that encloses the zoo entrance area; when doing so, make sure you put a set of attractions, conveniences, and food/drink stands right after bridge. You won't be able to stick to building restaurants in this scenario; the happiness boost provided by ice cream stands and burger shacks is too important. In addition, you'll need many "emergency" vending machines scattered in pairs here and there to keep guest hunger and thirst at bay (see Figure 8.10).

NOTE

"Tropical Rainforest Zoo" is 36 months long, and you'll make many hundreds of thousands of dollars. Money isn't likely to be a problem; spending it wisely might be.

FIGURE 8.10:
You'll need to provide numerous guest amenities to win this scenario.

Although you don't need to complete any research in order to win, completing selected programs can be helpful. It's not a bad idea to research Animal Houses early on; cash flows nicely in this scenario, so consider initiating research at minimum funding from the very start of the game. As you add exhibits, the number of zoo guests will keep increasing, which may lead to a drop in average guest happiness. You may be forced to raise the admission price sharply in order to thin the crowds out.

Plan the path network with great care. The paths forming the entrance crossways should be treated as the main traffic arteries in your zoo; you should try to expand simultaneously in all three directions (toward the center of the zoo area, left of the entrance, and right of the entrance). Lopsided development can throw traffic flow off balance, with guests crowding into the most developed area while the others stand empty.

TIP

Don't forget about zoo aesthetics; this scenario requires meaningful investments in zoo scenery. You should also consider building several Happiness Streets—paths lined with happiness-boosting buildings, decorative fencing, and beautiful zoo scenery.

Very Advanced Scenarios

There are only two scenarios in this group. However, both are long and difficult, so you needn't feel you're being shortchanged in terms of gameplay. The very last scenario, "Breeding Giant Pandas," is especially difficult. It doesn't require you to take a whole new approach or learn a multitude of new things; instead, it is a final exam on all your tycoon skills, requiring you to do everything exactly right and very, very fast.

Paradise Island

Starting money: $50,000

Winning conditions: Achieve a zoo rating of 80 or better, an average animal happiness of at least 95, an average guest happiness of 93+, and a suitability of at least 85 for all zoo exhibits.

Time: 36 months

Comments: You're not able to choose animals for adoption in this scenario; they'll all be donated, just as in "Forest Zoo," and the Adopt Animal button will be disabled. Remember that you can check on an animal's favorite foliage type by clicking the Animal Information button on the Zookeeper's Recommendations panel.

Just like the previous scenario, "Paradise Island" stresses tycoon talent number one: making lots of money fast. The zoo grounds are pretty small compared with the preceding scenarios, and bulldozing everything will yield just $16,700. The emergency grant of $10,000 comes in very handy!

You'll see immediately that building a zoo here requires far-reaching adjustments to the terrain within zoo walls. The zoo entrance is sunk in a deep little valley; the most cost-effective approach is to raise the zoo entrance until it's level with the large flat area to one side of the zoo gate (when looking at the gate from within the zoo, this area's to the right). When viewed from the front, the zoo gate will appear to be perched atop a high cliff (see Figure 8.11), but don't worry, guests will still arrive—they materialize on the tile right next to the entrance.

FIGURE 8.11:
Making the area around the entrance beautiful helps quickly raise new guests' happiness levels. The snowmen and the Christmas tree are scenery options available only around Christmastime.

Having raised the zoo entrance, smooth out all the dips, crevices, and mounds to create a large flat expanse on one side of the entrance. The other side features hills that are useful for the purpose of building a Siberian tiger exhibit. All the animals donated in this scenario arrive in pairs; make the exhibits bigger accordingly. The first set includes a pair of Siberian tigers, a couple of leopards, and two Bengal tigers; build the exhibits for the tigers and the leopards on the other side of the zoo entrance from the Siberian tiger exhibit, employing the zoo boundary as an exhibit barrier. The terrain adjustments you've made will have caused the outer zoo wall to disappear from view, but the zoo boundary still acts as a barrier; you don't need to spend money on fencing there. Laying out the exhibits in the described manner will allow you to get by with just a single zookeeper for the three exhibits; of course, as the scenario deadline approaches, you'll want to hire more zookeepers for the purpose of pouncing on any evil poo that might decrease exhibit suitability and, perish the thought, lose you the scenario.

The second set of animals will appear by the zoo gate the moment you bring the first three exhibits to an acceptable level. Don't spend money on more exhibits at this point; build an animal theater and a carousel, and add a restaurant and a compost building after the first month. Concentrate on making the exhibits better; it's easy to get the Golden Plaque for Excellence in Exhibit Design for the Bengal tiger exhibit. This comes with $15,000, giving a nice boost to your expansion effort.

> **TIP**
>
> *Consider allocating the minimum funding to researching Animal Shelters right from the start of the scenario. You need to complete all available research programs to win this scenario; note that Endangered Animals (Conservation) is not an option.*

Continue to expand your zoo in the standard manner, adding an attraction for each new exhibit. You need a high level of guest happiness for victory, so build ice cream stands and burger shacks even if your restaurants (you'll end up having two or three) are satisfying all guest needs—adults get a kick out of burger shacks, children from ice cream stands. You'll continue to receive new sets of animals every time you house the ones you've got in good exhibits. The second set consists of pairs of black bears, grizzly bears, and black leopards; it's convenient to put all the bears adjacent to the Siberian tigers, and the black leopards near the tigers and the leopards. The third set features a pair of moose and two elephants. Make sure the elephant exhibit is big enough. It's not easy to achieve high exhibit suitability for elephants: their favorite baobab trees take up a full tile each, and you should definitely research Large Elephant Shelter and Swinging Log Toy.

The fourth set of animals consists of just a pair of flamingos; they fit well next to the elephants. The fifth set consists of two saltwater crocodiles, and the sixth and final set is a pair giant pandas! Do not attempt to place the pandas in an exhibit until you've researched Bamboo (Exhibit Foliage) and Panda Cave (Animal Shelters). Animal Antibiotics (Animal Care) help keep these frail species healthy.

Thereafter, it's a question of tweaking your zoo to perfection in order to maintain high levels of happiness. Add guest amenities and zoo scenery, and don't forget to build a full set of animal houses featuring advanced exhibits. As usual, you might have to raise admission prices a few months before the end of the scenario to ensure a high level of guest happiness. Completing this scenario unlocks Mystery Beast #1; it's subsequently available in all *Zoo Tycoon* games.

BREEDING GIANT PANDAS

Starting money: $75,000

Winning conditions: Achieve a suitability of at least 90 for 15 zoo exhibits, and induce the giant pandas to reproduce in your zoo.

Time: 36 months

Comments: This is the big one! You begin Zoo Tycoon's last scenario with several zoo buildings and an entrance crossway. Although it looks very pretty, it's better that you bulldoze everything and build from scratch: The crossway is a little too far from the gate, and most of the existing concessions will lose heavy coin in the first month of operation. Customer happiness is not a concern in this scenario, which is just as well; you'll find yourself incredibly stretched financially.

The first reason for this is that you must build 15 very good exhibits on completely flat, grassy terrain; every exhibit, except perhaps the American bison's, will be expensive. In addition, you'll have to do a lot of research, and do it fairly fast. The only field where you can skip a couple of programs is Staff Education—you will neither need nor be able to afford tour guides in this scenario, so stop Staff Education research after completing first levels of zookeeper and maintenance worker training.

NOTE

In order to win, you must research a scenario-specific field named Panda Care. It consists of three lengthy and expensive programs, so you really cannot afford to waste time and money on research that isn't necessary for victory in this scenario.

You should begin by adopting only animals that don't need companions, giving preference to those with high foliage requirements. This is because it's easier to build excellent exhibits when you can plant two or four of the trees favored by the exhibited animal in a single terrain tile; you should make a point of getting the Golden Plaque for Excellence in Exhibit Design solely to collect the attached $15,000. Bulldozing all zoo structures and objects right at the start will yield just $9,600; if you count the emergency grant of $10,000, you'll have under $95,000 in starting cash. This is enough to kick off things by building five exhibits, siting them along the zoo walls to save a few dollars. You should also build an animal theater, two carousels, and a compost building right away, following with a restaurant a month later.

Be aware that this scenario requires you to build a very efficient money machine, and that you won't be able to win without having at least two animal theaters, three restaurants, and four carousels in addition to many food and drink stands and shacks. You should allow for the double-laning of the main paths halfway through the scenario (see Figure 8.12), as your zoo will have to accommodate 700-plus guests through most of the game; don't forget to leave space for a gift shop near the zoo entrance. In addition, you should have gift stands set up on every major corner.

WARNING

Building exhibits big enough to hold animal families may prove too expensive in this scenario, and mixed-species exhibits are ruled out by the high exhibit suitability required for victory.

Expansion is quickest if you continue building exhibits adjacent to the zoo wall. You should consider exhibiting solitary animals when possible. You don't have all 36 months to build the 15 required exhibits, either—you should allow the pandas at least six months to reproduce.

FIGURE 8.12:

Make sure your path network can handle heavy traffic, and place moneymaking structures on practically every corner.

All in all this means building 16 very good exhibits (the required 15 plus the pandas') in 30 months; the panda exhibit alone will cost you as much as two others—you need to build a large, absolutely perfect habitat. Naturally, as you build the exhibits you'll have to keep adding new moneymaking structures; monthly employee wages and zoo upkeep costs will reach the neighborhood of $10,000 a month. Expect to provide plenty of assistance to bewildered maintenance workers and harried zookeepers!

Do not spend any money on zoo aesthetics in this scenario until you're well into the second half of the scenario and are absolutely sure you have money to burn. Victory unlocks *Zoo Tycoon*'s second Mystery Beast, subsequently available in all scenarios.

ANIMAL FACTS

THE TABLE BELOW CONTAINS INDIVIDUAL ANIMAL DATA THAT IS HELPFUL WHEN MAKING EXHIBIT SIZE DECISIONS. THE DATA GO BEYOND THE MINIMUM NUMBER OF TILES PER ANIMAL AND THE MINIMUM AND MAXIMUM NUMBER OF ANIMALS ALLOWED INSIDE THE EXHIBIT. CAPTIVITY CHANCE REFERS TO THE AMOUNT OF HAPPINESS LOST WHEN AN ANIMAL REALIZES IT'S IN A ZOO, AND SICK CHANCE REPRESENTS THE PERCENTAGE PROBABILITY AN ANIMAL WILL FALL ILL WHEN THE GAME RUNS A HEALTH CHECK. REPRODUCTION HAPPINESS INDICATES WHAT LEVEL OF HAPPINESS MUST BE ACHIEVED FOR SUCCESSFUL BREEDING, WHILE REPRODUCTION CHANCE INDICATES THE CHANCES OF OFFSPRING APPEARING WHEN THE GAME RUNS A FERTILITY CHECK. THE FINAL COLUMN LISTS THE NUMBER OF OFFSPRING IF REPRODUCTION IS SUCCESSFUL.

NOTE THAT SICK CHANCE AND REPRODUCTION CHANCE MAY BE MODIFIED IN YOUR FAVOR AFTER RESEARCHING APPROPRIATE PROGRAMS (SEE CHAPTER 5).

SPECIES	SPACE PER ANIMAL	MIN/MAX ANIMALS	CAPTIVITY CHANCE	SICK CHANCE	REPRODUCTION HAPPINESS	REPRODUCTION CHANCE	OFFSPRING
AFRICAN BUFFALO	20	2/10	5	5	90	2	1
AMERICAN BIGHORN SHEEP	20	3/10	5	12	85	3	1
AMERICAN BISON	20	3/10	5	10	85	2	1
ANTEATER	15	1/3	5	5	90	2	1
ARCTIC WOLF	35	4/20	8	3	85	2	2
BABOON	15	3/20	10	12	85	2	1
BENGAL TIGER	35	1/2	2	5	85	3	2
BLACK BEAR	35	1/3	10	10	85	2	2
BLACK LEOPARD	20	1/2	7	8	95	1	1
BLACK RHINO	50	1/2	5	5	90	2	1
CALIFORNIA SEA LION	35	2/16	5	5	90	2	1
CHEETAH	50	1/3	12	15	95	1	1
CHIMPANZEE	15	3/15	10	12	85	3	1
CLOUDED LEOPARD	35	1/2	10	8	95	2	1
COMMON WILDEBEEST	15	3/25	5	10	90	3	1
DROMEDARY CAMEL	20	1/10	5	10	85	2	1
ELEPHANT	50	2/6	10	2	95	1	1
EMPEROR PENGUIN	15	2/16	5	5	90	2	1
GEMSBOK	20	3/15	5	3	90	3	1
GIANT PANDA	20	1/2	15	40	97	1	1
GIRAFFE	35	2/10	12	5	95	2	1
GRAY WOLF	35	4/20	8	3	85	3	2
GREATER FLAMINGO	15	2/20	7	5	90	2	2
GRIZZLY BEAR	50	1/3	10	10	85	1	2
HIPPOPOTAMUS	35	2/10	5	5	90	2	1
HYENA	20	3/15	5	10	90	2	2
IBEX	20	3/10	5	5	85	2	1
JAGUAR	20	1/2	7	12	95	1	1
LEOPARD	35	1/2	7	8	90	2	2
LION	20	3/10	2	5	85	3	2
LOWLAND GORILLA	20	2/10	12	15	95	1	1
MANDRILL	15	3/20	10	15	85	2	1
MARKHOR	20	2/7	10	10	85	2	1
MOOSE	20	1/3	5	10	90	2	1
OKAPI	20	1/2	15	12	95	1	1

SPECIES	SPACE PER ANIMAL	MIN/MAX ANIMALS	CAPTIVITY CHANCE	SICK CHANCE	REPRODUCTION HAPPINESS	REPRODUCTION CHANCE	OFFSPRING
OSTRICH	20	2/12	10	8	90	2	2
POLAR BEAR	35	1/3	10	10	90	2	2
RED KANGAROO	20	1/3	8	5	95	3	1
SNOW LEOPARD	35	1/2	13	10	90	1	1
SIBERIAN TIGER	35	2/3	2	10	85	3	2
SALTWATER CROCODILE	20	2/3	5	5	93	2	2
THOMPSON'S GAZELLE	15	3/25	2	5	85	3	1
WARTHOG	20	2/6	5	5	90	2	3
WHITE BENGAL TIGER	35	2/3	2	10	90	1	1
ZEBRA	15	3/20	5	12	90	3	1

HIS TABLE LISTS ZOO BUILDING AND ZOO ITEM DATA. NOTE THAT BUILDINGS SELLING FOOD AND DRINK ITEMS MAY PROVIDE A DOUBLE HAPPINESS BOOST: FIRST WHEN A ZOO GUEST BUYS AN ITEM, AND AGAIN WHEN THE FOOD OR DRINK BOUGHT IS CONSUMED. THE FOUR LAST COLUMNS LIST THE CHANGE TO ZOO GUEST NEEDS THAT RESULTS FROM "USING" A BUILDING OR CONSUMING AN ITEM.

BUILDING	CONSTRUC-TION/ MONTHLY UPKEEP COST	CAPACITY	ADULT HAPPINESS CHANGE	CHILD HAPPINESS CHANGE	—AESTHETIC VALUE—			
					MAN	WOMAN	BOY	GIRL
BURGER SHACK	$250	3	10					
HOT DOG STAND	$175	2						
PIZZA SHACK	$325	6						
CANDY VENDING MACHINE	$50	1						
ICE CREAM STAND	$125	2	5	15			10	10
RESTAURANT	$1,000	12	15		10	10		
DRINKSTAND	$200	4	5	5				
SODA VENDING MACHINE	$50	1						
RESTROOM	$120	2	5	5	-5	-5	-5	-5
FAMILY RESTROOM	$250	8	20	20				
GIFT SHOP	$600	12	8	15				
GIFT STAND	$125	1	5	5			5	5
AVIARY	$1,600	12	15		15	15		
PRIMATE HOUSE	$1,100	8	5	20	10		15	15
REPTILE HOUSE	$950	6	5	10		10		
INSECT HOUSE	$600	4		15		10		
JAPANESE GARDEN	$1,900	4	30	10	25	25	10	10
ANIMAL THEATER	$1,300	12	12	8	10	10		
ELEPHANT RIDE	$1,200	2	3	20	-5	-5	10	10
CAROUSEL	$800	12		12	10	10	20	20
PETTING ZOO	$700	4	10	15	5	5	15	15
COMPOST BUILDING	$1,500				-25	-25	-25	-25

BUILDING	SALE ITEM	ADULT HAPPINESS CHANGE	CHILD HAPPINESS CHANGE	HUNGER CHANGE	THIRST CHANGE	RESTROOM NEED CHANGE	ENERGY CHANGE
BURGER SHACK	Burger	20	10	-100	10		
HOT DOG STAND	Hot dog	10	10	-50	15		
PIZZA SHACK	Pizza	10	15	-150	15		
CANDY VENDING MACHINE	Candy	5	15	-15			
ICE CREAM STAND	Ice Cream	15	30	-15	5		-20
RESTAURANT	(all guest amenities)			-200	-200	-200	-100
DRINKSTAND	Soda	10	10		-100	20	
SODA VENDING MACHINE	Soda can	10	10		-25	10	15
RESTROOM						-100	
FAMILY RESTROOM						-200	
GIFT SHOP							
GIFT STAND							
AVIARY							
PRIMATE HOUSE							
REPTILE HOUSE							
INSECT HOUSE							
JAPANESE GARDEN							-50
ANIMAL THEATER							
ELEPHANT RIDE							
CAROUSEL							
PETTING ZOO							
COMPOST BUILDING							

THIS TABLE LISTS ALL ZOO STRUCTURES AND OBJECTS THAT HAVE AN AESTHETIC VALUE. NOTE THAT OBJECTS WITH AN AESTHETIC VALUE ARE PRESENT IN SEVERAL OF THE GAME MENUS: FLOWERBEDS APPEAR IN THE FOLIAGE MENU, BUT OBSERVATION AREAS APPEAR UNDER ZOO SCENERY, ETC. THE FLOWERBEDS IN THE TABLE ARE LISTED IN THE SAME ORDER AS IN THE GAME MENU.

NOTE THAT ONLY A SELECT FEW TREES HAVE AESTHETIC VALUE; SELECTING OTHER TREE TYPES FOR LANDSCAPING MIGHT PLEASE YOU, BUT ZOO GUESTS WON'T CARE. FINALLY, YOU SHOULD KNOW THAT THIS TABLE DOES NOT LIST THE GAME'S "HIDDEN" ZOO SCENERY OBJECTS. MAKE SURE YOU EXAMINE THE ZOO SCENERY MENU AROUND HALLOWEEN AND AT CHRISTMASTIME! YOU'LL SEE A WITCH FLY OVER YOUR ZOO ASTRIDE A BROOM ON THE FIRST OCCASION, AND WILL BE VISITED BY SANTA CLAUS ON THE SECOND.

OBJECT	COST	MAN	WOMAN	BOY	GIRL
TRASH	-	-15	-15	-15	-15
TRASHCAN	$25	-10	-10	-10	-10
EXHIBIT INFO SIGN	$50	4	4	2	2
LAMP	$65	3	3	-	-
HEDGE	$100	3	3	-	-
OBSERVATION AREA - METAL	$150	2	2	2	2
OBSERVATION AREA - STICK	$175	3	3	3	3
LION STATUE	$185	6	3	6	3
OBSERVATION AREA - WOOD	$200	2	4	2	4
OBSERVATION AREA - GRATE	$200	4	2	4	2
ELEPHANT STATUE	$210	3	6	3	6
FOUNTAIN	$250	5	5	5	5
ZOO MAP	$250	8	8	5	5
OBSERVATION AREA - CONCRETE	$250	8	4	8	4
OBSERVATION AREA - ROCK	$250	4	4	8	8
BIGHORN STATUE	$450	8	8	8	8
ELEPHANT FOUNTAIN	$500	6	6	10	10
TURTLE FOUNTAIN	$800	15	15	15	15
SMALL FLOWERBED 1	$40	2	4	2	4
SMALL FLOWERBED 2	$40	4	4	2	2
SMALL FLOWERBED 3	$40	2	2	4	4
SMALL FLOWERBED 4	$40	4	2	4	2
BIG FLOWERBED 1	$80	8	4	8	4
BIG FLOWERBED 2	$80	4	8	4	8
BIG FLOWERBED 3	$80	4	4	8	8
WILD OLIVE TREE	$120	2	2	2	2
PACIFIC DOGWOOD TREE	$125	3	3	3	3
JAPANESE MAPLE TREE	$135	6	6	3	3
SPIRAL TOPIARY	$150	5	5	-	-
CHERRY TREE	$175	8	8	4	4
GIRAFFE TOPIARY	$200	3	3	6	6
BEAR TOPIARY	$200	6	3	6	3
RHINO TOPIARY	$200	4	2	4	2
ELEPHANT TOPIARY	$225	3	6	3	6
DUCK POND	$500	10	10	15	15
HEDGE	$100	5	5	5	5

OBJECT	COST	MAN	WOMAN	BOY	GIRL
POST AND ROPE FENCE	$30	5	5	5	5
PICKET FENCE	$30	5	10	5	10
WHITE FENCE	$60	5	5	10	10
CAST IRON FENCE	$65	10	5	10	5
BRICK WALL	$80	10	10	10	10
LOW HEDGE FENCE	$85	5	5	5	5
BATHROOM	$120	-5	-5	-5	-5
GIFT STAND	$125	-	-	5	5
ICE CREAM STAND	$125	-	-	10	10
INSECT HOUSE	$600	-	-	10	-
PETTING ZOO	$700	5	5	15	15
CAROUSEL	$800	10	10	20	20
REPTILE HOUSE	$950	-	-	10	-
RESTAURANT	$1,000	10	10	-	-
PRIMATE HOUSE	$1,100	10	-	15	15
ELEPHANT RIDE	$1,200	-5	-5	10	10
ANIMAL THEATRE	$1,300	10	10	-	-
COMPOST BUILDING	$1,500	-25	-25	-25	-25
AVIARY	$1,600	15	15	-	-
JAPANESE GARDEN	$1,900	25	25	10	10
DIRT PATH	$10	2	2	2	2
SAND PATH	$10	2	2	2	2
CONCRETE PATH	$25	4	4	4	4
ASPHALT PATH	$25	4	4	4	4
BRICK PATH	$50	6	6	6	6
STONE PATH	$50	6	6	6	6

ANIMAL
COMPATIBILITY

This table lists compatible animal species. However, species that like each other can have different habitat requirements, so make sure you consult the relevant animal portraits in Chapter 3 before making a final decision.

	AFRICAN BUFFALO	ANTEATER	BABOON	BIGHORN SHEEP	BISON
AFRICAN BUFFALO	X	-	-	-	-
ANTEATER	-	X	-	-	-
BABOON	-	-	X	-	-
BIGHORN SHEEP	-	-	-	X	X
BISON	-	-	-	X	X
BLACK BEAR	-	-	-	-	-
BLACK LEOPARD	-	-	-	-	-
BLACK RHINO	X	-	-	-	-
CHEETAH	-	-	-	-	-
CHIMPANZEE	-	-	-	-	-
CLOULDED LEOPARD	-	-	-	-	-
DROMEDARY CAMEL	-	-	-	-	-
ELEPHANT	X	-	-	-	-
EMPEROR PENGUIN	-	-	-	-	-
FLAMINGO, GREATER	X	-	-	-	-
GAZELLE, THOMSON'S	X	-	-	-	-
GEMSBOK	X	-	-	-	-
GIRAFFE	X	-	-	-	-
GORILLA, LOWLAND	-	-	-	-	-
GRAY WOLF	-	-	-	-	-
GRIZZLY BEAR	-	-	-	-	-
HIPPOPOTAMUS	X	-	-	-	-
HYENA	-	-	-	-	-
IBEX	-	-	-	-	-
JAGUAR	-	-	-	-	-
KANGAROO, RED	-	-	-	-	-
LEOPARD	-	-	-	-	-
LION	-	-	-	-	-
MANDRILL	-	-	X	-	-
MARKHOR	-	-	-	-	-
MOOSE	-	-	-	X	X
OKAPI	X	-	-	-	-
OSTRICH	X	-	-	-	-
PANDA	-	-	-	-	-
POLAR BEAR	-	-	-	-	-
SEA LION, CALIFORNIA	-	-	-	-	-
SNOW LEOPARD	-	-	-	-	-
SIBERIAN TIGER	-	-	-	-	-
SALTWATER CROCODILE	-	-	-	-	-
BENGAL TIGER	-	-	-	-	-
WARTHOG	X	-	-	-	-
WILDEBEEST, COMMON	X	-	-	-	-
WHITE BENGAL TIGER	-	-	-	-	-
ZEBRA	X	-	-	-	-

	BLACK BEAR	BLACK LEOPARD	BLACK RHINO	CHEETAH	CHIMPANZEE
AFRICAN BUFFALO	-	-	X	-	-
ANTEATER	-	-	-	-	-
BABOON	-	-	-	-	-
BIGHORN SHEEP	-	-	-	-	-
BISON	-	-	-	-	-
BLACK BEAR	X	-	-	-	-
BLACK LEOPARD	-	X	-	-	-
BLACK RHINO	-	-	X	-	-
CHEETAH	-	-	-	X	-
CHIMPANZEE	-	-	-	-	X
CLOULDED LEOPARD	-	X	-	-	-
DROMEDARY CAMEL	-	-	-	-	-
ELEPHANT	-	-	-	-	-
EMPEROR PENGUIN	-	-	-	-	-
FLAMINGO, GREATER	-	-	X	-	-
GAZELLE, THOMSON'S	-	-	X	-	-
GEMSBOK	-	-	X	-	-
GIRAFFE	-	-	X	-	-
GORILLA, LOWLAND	-	-	-	-	X
GRAY WOLF	-	-	-	-	-
GRIZZLY BEAR	X	-	-	-	-
HIPPOPOTAMUS	-	-	X	-	-
HYENA	-	-	-	-	-
IBEX	-	-	-	-	-
JAGUAR	-	-	-	-	-
KANGAROO, RED	-	-	-	-	-
LEOPARD	-	-	-	-	-
LION	-	-	-	-	-
MANDRILL	-	-	-	-	-
MARKHOR	-	-	-	-	-
MOOSE	-	-	-	-	-
OKAPI	-	-	X	-	-
OSTRICH	-	-	X	-	-
PANDA	-	-	-	-	-
POLAR BEAR	X	-	-	-	-
SEA LION, CALIFORNIA	-	-	-	-	-
SNOW LEOPARD	-	-	-	-	-
SIBERIAN TIGER	-	-	-	-	-
SALTWATER CROCODILE	-	-	-	-	-
BENGAL TIGER	-	-	-	-	-
WARTHOG	-	-	X	-	-
WILDEBEEST, COMMON	-	-	X	-	-
WHITE BENGAL TIGER	-	-	-	-	-
ZEBRA	-	-	X	-	-

ANIMAL COMPATIBILITY

	CLOULDED LEOPARD	DROMEDARY CAMEL	ELEPHANT	EMPEROR PENGUIN	FLAMINGO, GREATER
AFRICAN BUFFALO	-	-	X	-	X
ANTEATER	-	-	-	-	-
BABOON	-	-	-	-	-
BIGHORN SHEEP	-	-	-	-	-
BISON	-	-	-	-	-
BLACK BEAR	-	-	-	-	-
BLACK LEOPARD	X	-	-	-	-
BLACK RHINO	-	-	X	-	X
CHEETAH	-	-	-	-	-
CHIMPANZEE	-	-	-	-	-
CLOULDED LEOPARD	X	-	-	-	-
DROMEDARY CAMEL	-	X	-	-	-
ELEPHANT	-	-	X	-	X
EMPEROR PENGUIN	-	-	-	X	-
FLAMINGO, GREATER	-	-	X	-	X
GAZELLE, THOMSON'S	-	-	X	-	X
GEMSBOK	-	X	X	-	X
GIRAFFE	-	-	X	-	X
GORILLA, LOWLAND	-	-	-	-	-
GRAY WOLF	-	-	-	-	-
GRIZZLY BEAR	-	-	-	-	-
HIPPOPOTAMUS	-	-	X	-	X
HYENA	-	-	-	-	-
IBEX	-	-	-	-	-
JAGUAR	-	-	-	-	-
KANGAROO, RED	-	-	-	-	-
LEOPARD	-	-	-	-	-
LION	-	-	-	-	-
MANDRILL	-	-	-	-	-
MARKHOR	-	-	-	-	-
MOOSE	-	-	-	-	-
OKAPI	-	-	X	-	X
OSTRICH	-	-	X	-	X
PANDA	-	-	-	-	-
POLAR BEAR	-	-	-	-	-
SEA LION, CALIFORNIA	-	-	-	X	-
SNOW LEOPARD	-	-	-	-	-
SIBERIAN TIGER	-	-	-	-	-
SALTWATER CROCODILE	-	-	-	-	-
BENGAL TIGER	-	-	-	-	-
WARTHOG	-	-	X	-	X
WILDEBEEST, COMMON	-	-	X	-	X
WHITE BENGAL TIGER	-	-	-	-	-
ZEBRA	-	-	X	-	X

	GAZELLE, THOMSON'S	GEMSBOK	GIRAFFE	GORILLA, LOWLAND	GRAY WOLF
AFRICAN BUFFALO	X	X	X	-	-
ANTEATER	-	-	-	-	-
BABOON	-	-	-	-	-
BIGHORN SHEEP	-	-	-	-	-
BISON	-	-	-	-	-
BLACK BEAR	-	-	-	-	-
BLACK LEOPARD	-	-	-	-	-
BLACK RHINO	X	X	X	-	-
CHEETAH	-	-	-	-	-
CHIMPANZEE	-	-	-	X	-
CLOULDED LEOPARD	-	-	-	-	-
DROMEDARY CAMEL	-	-	-	-	-
ELEPHANT	X	X	X	-	-
EMPEROR PENGUIN	-	-	-	-	-
FLAMINGO, GREATER	X	X	X	-	-
GAZELLE, THOMSON'S	X	X	X	-	-
GEMSBOK	X	X	X	-	-
GIRAFFE	X	X	X	-	-
GORILLA, LOWLAND	-	-	-	X	-
GRAY WOLF	-	-	-	-	X
GRIZZLY BEAR	-	-	-	-	-
HIPPOPOTAMUS	X	X	X	-	-
HYENA	-	-	-	-	-
IBEX	-	-	-	-	-
JAGUAR	-	-	-	-	-
KANGAROO, RED	-	-	-	-	-
LEOPARD	-	-	-	-	-
LION	-	-	-	-	-
MANDRILL	-	-	-	-	-
MARKHOR	-	-	-	-	-
MOOSE	-	-	-	-	-
OKAPI	X	X	X	-	-
OSTRICH	X	X	X	-	-
PANDA	-	-	-	-	-
POLAR BEAR	-	-	-	-	-
SEA LION, CALIFORNIA	-	-	-	-	-
SNOW LEOPARD	-	-	-	-	-
SIBERIAN TIGER	-	-	-	-	-
SALTWATER CROCODILE	-	-	-	-	-
BENGAL TIGER	-	-	-	-	-
WARTHOG	X	X	X	-	-
WILDEBEEST, COMMON	X	X	X	-	-
WHITE BENGAL TIGER	-	-	-	-	-
ZEBRA	X	X	X	-	-

	GRIZZLY BEAR	HIPPO-POTAMUS	HYENA	IBEX	JAGUAR
AFRICAN BUFFALO	-	X	-	-	-
ANTEATER	-	-	-	-	-
BABOON	-	-	-	-	-
BIGHORN SHEEP	-	-	-	-	-
BISON	-	-	-	-	-
BLACK BEAR	X	-	-	-	-
BLACK LEOPARD	-	-	-	-	-
BLACK RHINO	-	X	-	-	-
CHEETAH	-	-	-	-	-
CHIMPANZEE	-	-	-	-	-
CLOULDED LEOPARD	-	-	-	-	-
DROMEDARY CAMEL	-	-	-	-	-
ELEPHANT	-	X	-	-	-
EMPEROR PENGUIN	-	-	-	-	-
FLAMINGO, GREATER	-	X	-	-	-
GAZELLE, THOMSON'S	-	X	-	-	-
GEMSBOK	-	X	-	-	-
GIRAFFE	-	X	-	-	-
GORILLA, LOWLAND	-	-	-	-	-
GRAY WOLF	-	-	-	-	-
GRIZZLY BEAR	X	-	-	-	-
HIPPOPOTAMUS	-	X	-	-	-
HYENA	-	-	X	-	-
IBEX	-	-	-	X	-
JAGUAR	-	-	-	-	X
KANGAROO, RED	-	-	-	-	-
LEOPARD	-	-	-	-	-
LION	-	-	-	-	-
MANDRILL	-	-	-	-	-
MARKHOR	-	-	-	X	-
MOOSE	-	-	-	-	-
OKAPI	-	X	-	-	-
OSTRICH	-	X	-	-	-
PANDA	-	-	-	-	-
POLAR BEAR	X	-	-	-	-
SEA LION, CALIFORNIA	-	-	-	-	-
SNOW LEOPARD	-	-	-	-	-
SIBERIAN TIGER	-	-	-	-	-
SALTWATER CROCODILE	-	-	-	-	-
BENGAL TIGER	-	-	-	-	-
WARTHOG	-	X	-	-	-
WILDEBEEST, COMMON	-	X	-	-	-
WHITE BENGAL TIGER	-	-	-	-	-
ZEBRA	-	X	-	-	-

	KANGAROO, RED	LEOPARD	LION	MANDRILL	MARKHOR
AFRICAN BUFFALO	-	-	-	-	-
ANTEATER	-	-	-	-	-
BABOON	-	-	-	X	-
BIGHORN SHEEP	-	-	-	-	-
BISON	-	-	-	-	-
BLACK BEAR	-	-	-	-	-
BLACK LEOPARD	-	-	-	-	-
BLACK RHINO	-	-	-	-	-
CHEETAH	-	-	-	-	-
CHIMPANZEE	-	-	-	-	-
CLOULDED LEOPARD	-	-	-	-	-
DROMEDARY CAMEL	-	-	-	-	-
ELEPHANT	-	-	-	-	-
EMPEROR PENGUIN	-	-	-	-	-
FLAMINGO, GREATER	-	-	-	-	-
GAZELLE, THOMSON'S	-	-	-	-	-
GEMSBOK	-	-	-	-	-
GIRAFFE	-	-	-	-	-
GORILLA, LOWLAND	-	-	-	-	-
GRAY WOLF	-	-	-	-	-
GRIZZLY BEAR	-	-	-	-	-
HIPPOPOTAMUS	-	-	-	-	-
HYENA	-	-	-	-	-
IBEX	-	-	-	-	X
JAGUAR	-	-	-	-	-
KANGAROO, RED	X	-	-	-	-
LEOPARD	-	X	-	-	-
LION	-	-	X	-	-
MANDRILL	-	-	-	X	-
MARKHOR	-	-	-	-	X
MOOSE	-	-	-	-	-
OKAPI	-	-	-	-	-
OSTRICH	-	-	-	-	-
PANDA	-	-	-	-	-
POLAR BEAR	-	-	-	-	-
SEA LION, CALIFORNIA	-	-	-	-	-
SNOW LEOPARD	-	-	-	-	-
SIBERIAN TIGER	-	-	-	-	-
SALTWATER CROCODILE	-	-	-	-	-
BENGAL TIGER	-	-	-	-	-
WARTHOG	-	-	-	-	-
WILDEBEEST, COMMON	-	-	-	-	-
WHITE BENGAL TIGER	-	-	-	-	-
ZEBRA	-	-	-	-	-

197

	MOOSE	OKAPI	OSTRICH	PANDA	POLAR BEAR
AFRICAN BUFFALO	-	X	X	-	-
ANTEATER	-	-	-	-	-
BABOON	-	-	-	-	-
BIGHORN SHEEP	X	-	-	-	-
BISON	X	-	-	-	-
BLACK BEAR	-	-	-	-	X
BLACK LEOPARD	-	-	-	-	-
BLACK RHINO	-	X	X	-	-
CHEETAH	-	-	-	-	-
CHIMPANZEE	-	-	-	-	-
CLOULDED LEOPARD	-	-	-	-	-
DROMEDARY CAMEL	-	-	-	-	-
ELEPHANT	-	X	X	-	-
EMPEROR PENGUIN	-	-	-	-	-
FLAMINGO, GREATER	-	X	X	-	-
GAZELLE, THOMSON'S	-	X	X	-	-
GEMSBOK	-	X	X	-	-
GIRAFFE	-	X	X	-	-
GORILLA, LOWLAND	-	-	-	-	-
GRAY WOLF	-	-	-	-	-
GRIZZLY BEAR	-	-	-	-	X
HIPPOPOTAMUS	-	X	X	-	-
HYENA	-	-	-	-	-
IBEX	-	-	-	-	-
JAGUAR	-	-	-	-	-
KANGAROO, RED	-	-	-	-	-
LEOPARD	-	-	-	-	-
LION	-	-	-	-	-
MANDRILL	-	-	-	-	-
MARKHOR	-	-	-	-	-
MOOSE	X	-	-	-	-
OKAPI	-	X	X	-	-
OSTRICH	-	X	X	-	-
PANDA	-	-	-	X	-
POLAR BEAR	-	-	-	-	X
SEA LION, CALIFORNIA	-	-	-	-	-
SNOW LEOPARD	-	-	-	-	-
SIBERIAN TIGER	-	-	-	-	-
SALTWATER CROCODILE	-	-	-	-	-
BENGAL TIGER	-	-	-	-	-
WARTHOG	-	X	X	-	-
WILDEBEEST, COMMON	-	X	X	-	-
WHITE BENGAL TIGER	-	-	-	-	-
ZEBRA	-	X	X	-	-

	SEA LION, CALIFORNIA	SNOW LEOPARD	SIBERIAN TIGER	SALTWATER CROCODILE	BENGAL TIGER
AFRICAN BUFFALO	-	-	-	-	-
ANTEATER	-	-	-	-	-
BABOON	-	-	-	-	-
BIGHORN SHEEP	-	-	-	-	-
BISON	-	-	-	-	-
BLACK BEAR	-	-	-	-	-
BLACK LEOPARD	-	-	-	-	-
BLACK RHINO	-	-	-	-	-
CHEETAH	-	-	-	-	-
CHIMPANZEE	-	-	-	-	-
CLOULDED LEOPARD	-	-	-	-	-
DROMEDARY CAMEL	-	-	-	-	-
ELEPHANT	-	-	-	-	-
EMPEROR PENGUIN	X	-	-	-	-
FLAMINGO, GREATER	-	-	-	-	-
GAZELLE, THOMSON'S	-	-	-	-	-
GEMSBOK	-	-	-	-	-
GIRAFFE	-	-	-	-	-
GORILLA, LOWLAND	-	-	-	-	-
GRAY WOLF	-	-	-	-	-
GRIZZLY BEAR	-	-	-	-	-
HIPPOPOTAMUS	-	-	-	-	-
HYENA	-	-	-	-	-
IBEX	-	-	-	-	-
JAGUAR	-	-	-	-	-
KANGAROO, RED	-	-	-	-	-
LEOPARD	-	-	-	-	-
LION	-	-	-	-	-
MANDRILL	-	-	-	-	-
MARKHOR	-	-	-	-	-
MOOSE	-	-	-	-	-
OKAPI	-	-	-	-	-
OSTRICH	-	-	-	-	-
PANDA	-	-	-	-	-
POLAR BEAR	-	-	-	-	-
SEA LION, CALIFORNIA	X	-	-	-	-
SNOW LEOPARD	-	X	-	-	-
SIBERIAN TIGER	-	-	X	-	-
SALTWATER CROCODILE	-	-	-	X	-
BENGAL TIGER	-	-	-	-	X
WARTHOG	-	-	-	-	-
WILDEBEEST, COMMON	-	-	-	-	-
WHITE BENGAL TIGER	-	-	-	-	X
ZEBRA	-	-	-	-	-

	WARTHOG	WILDEBEEST, COMMON	WHITE BENGAL TIGER	ZEBRA
AFRICAN BUFFALO	X	X		X
ANTEATER	-	-	-	-
BABOON	-	-	-	-
BIGHORN SHEEP	-	-	-	-
BISON	-	-	-	-
BLACK BEAR	-	-	-	-
BLACK LEOPARD	-	-	-	-
BLACK RHINO	X	X	-	X
CHEETAH	-	-	-	-
CHIMPANZEE	-	-	-	-
CLOULDED LEOPARD	-	-	-	-
DROMEDARY CAMEL	-	-	-	-
ELEPHANT	X	X	-	X
EMPEROR PENGUIN	-	-	-	-
FLAMINGO, GREATER	X	X	-	X
GAZELLE, THOMSON'S	X	X	-	X
GEMSBOK	X	X	-	X
GIRAFFE	X	X	-	X
GORILLA, LOWLAND	-	-	-	-
GRAY WOLF	-	-	-	-
GRIZZLY BEAR	-	-	-	-
HIPPOPOTAMUS	X	X	-	X
HYENA	-	-	-	-
IBEX	-	-	-	-
JAGUAR	-	-	-	-
KANGAROO, RED	-	-	-	-
LEOPARD	-	-	-	-
LION	-	-	-	-
MANDRILL	-	-	-	-
MARKHOR	-	-	-	-
MOOSE	-	-	-	-
OKAPI	X	X	-	X
OSTRICH	X	X	-	X
PANDA	-	-	-	-
POLAR BEAR	-	-	-	-
SEA LION, CALIFORNIA	-	-	-	-
SNOW LEOPARD	-	-	-	-
SIBERIAN TIGER	-	-	-	-
SALTWATER CROCODILE	-	-	-	-
BENGAL TIGER	-	-	X	-
WARTHOG	X	X	-	X
WILDEBEEST, COMMON	X	X	-	X
WHITE BENGAL TIGER	-	-	X	-
ZEBRA	X	X	-	X